Medieval History-Based Writing Lessons

Structure, Style, Grammar & Vocabulary

Teacher's Manual

by Lori Verstegen

Fourth Edition © February 2016
Institute for Excellence in Writing, L.L.C.

Also by Lori Verstegen

Advanced U.S. History-Based Writing Lessons
All Things Fun and Fascinating
Ancient History-Based Writing Lessons
Bible Heroes Writing Lessons
Dress-Ups, Decorations, and Delightful Diversions
Medieval History-Based Writing Lessons (Student Book)
Student Resource Notebook
U.S. History-Based Writing Lessons, Vol. 1: Explorers to the Gold Rush

The purchase of this book entitles its owner to a free downloadable copy of the *Student Resource Notebook*, the *Medieval History-Based Advanced Writing Lessons Blackline Masters*, and the *Advanced Writing Lessons Sample Key Word Outlines*.

Go to IEW.com/MHW-E. (See the blue page for complete download instructions.)

Institute for Excellence in Writing (IEW®)
8799 N. 387 Road
Locust Grove, OK 74352
800.856.5815
info@IEW.com   IEW.com

Printed in the United States of America

IEW® is a registered trademark of the Institute for Excellence in Writing, L.L.C.

Accessing Your Downloads

The purchase of this book entitles its owner to a free download of the following:

- *Student Resource Notebook* (114 pages*)
- the optional *Medieval History-Based Advanced Writing Lessons Blackline* Masters e-book (20 pages)
- the optional *Advanced Writing Lessons Sample Key Word Outlines* e-book (20 pages)

To download these e-resources, please follow the directions below:

1. Go to our website: IEW.com
2. Log in to your online customer account. If you do not have an account, you will need to create one.
3. After you are logged in, go to this web page: IEW.com/MHW-E
4. Click the red arrow, and then click the checkboxes next to the names of the files you wish to place in your account.
5. Click the "Add to my files" button.
6. To access your files now and in the future, click on "Your Account," and click on the "Files" tab (one of the gray tabs).
7. Click on each file name to download the files onto your computer.

Please note: You are free to download and print these e-books as needed for use within *your immediate family or classroom*. However, this information is proprietary, and we are trusting you to be on your honor not to share it with anyone. Please see the copyright page for further details. Thank you.

* If you would prefer to purchase *Student Resource Notebook* as a preprinted, spiral-bound book, it is available at this web page: IEW.com/SRN-B

If you have any difficulty receiving these downloads after going through the steps above, please call 800.856.5815.

Institute for Excellence in Writing
8799 N. 387 Road
Locust Grove, OK 74352

Contents

Inventive Writing (IEW Unit 7)

Formal Essay Models (IEW Unit 8)

Formal Critique and Response to Literature (IEW Unit 9)

Formal Essay Model with Library Research (IEW Unit 8)

Just for Fun

Appendices

Welcome to *Medieval History-Based Writing Lessons in Structure and Style*. This Teacher's Manual now includes inset Student Book pages. Instructions to teachers, sample answers to questions, sample key word outlines, brainstorming ideas, review games, and helps for motivating students are inserted. This format allows a teacher to teach directly from the Teacher's Manual without the need of her own copy of the Student Book.

Teachers, please read the introduction before the first day of class. Ask parents to have the *Student Resource Notebook* (SRN) ready for Lesson 1. On the first day of class, summarize the introductory information with your students. Then proceed to Lesson 1.

Lesson instructions in the Student Book are directed to the student, but teachers should read over them with their students and help as necessary, especially with outlining and brainstorming. It is assumed that teachers have attended IEW's *Teaching Writing: Structure and Style* seminar, either live or on DVD, and own the *Seminar Workbook*. Before each new unit, teachers should review the appropriate information in that workbook.

Introduction

The lessons in this book teach structure and style in writing. As they move through medieval history themes, they incrementally introduce and review most of the models of structure and elements of style found in the Institute for Excellence in Writing's *Teaching Writing: Structure and Style*.

Student Book Contents

- **A Scope and Sequence Chart** (pages 8–9)

- **The Lesson Pages**
  This is the majority of the text. It contains the instructions, source texts, worksheets, and checklists you will need for each lesson.

- **Appendix 1: Modified MLA Format**

- **Appendix 2: Polished Draft Notebook and Keepsake**
  This appendix explains the polished draft notebook and includes a checklist that may be copied and used if teachers require these drafts to be turned in for grading.

- **Appendix 3: Student Samples**
  At least one student sample for each of the IEW units is included to help clarify instructions and inspire you.

  > It would be very helpful to have students tab each appendix. Ask them to bring sticky tabs to the first class.

- **Appendix 4: Adding Literature**
  This appendix suggests various classic novels set in the Middle Ages to be read alongside the writing lessons. It also includes masters of literature response pages if teachers would like to assign such pages for students adding the literature reading. These great stories will enhance the students' understanding of medieval times as well as provide background for the compositions they will write for these lessons.

- **Appendix 5: Vocabulary Chart, Quizzes, and Cards**
  The vocabulary words are an important part of these lessons. You will be instructed to cut out one set of cards for some of the lessons. You should include some of these words in each composition you write. You will also be quizzed over the words periodically. The goal is that these great words will become part of your natural writing vocabulary.

Medieval History-Based Advanced Writing Lessons Blackline Masters
These optional more advanced source texts, along with a few suggestions for more advanced structure and style—to be done in addition to some of the regular lessons—will help keep veteran IEW students progressing.

> The Teacher's Manual does not include a set of cards. The chart includes all the words with their definitions.

Medieval History-Based Advanced Writing Lessons Sample Key Word Outlines
Sample key word outlines for the advanced source texts are available (see the blue page).

This Teacher's Manual includes an additional **Appendix 6: Motivating Students: Tickets and Games**. Some games require a little preparation, so be sure to read the Teacher's Manual a few days before class. Many games require the use of dice, so be sure to have some.

Teacher's Manual

The Teacher's Manual includes all of the above (except the vocabulary cards) with added instructions for teachers, including sample key word outlines and brainstorming ideas, answers to questions, answers to vocabulary quizzes, and an additional Appendix 6. This appendix includes ideas for motivating students, such as using tickets and games. Teachers may teach directly from this manual without the need of their own copy of the Student Book.

Checklists

Each lesson includes a checklist that details all the requirements of the assignment for you and your teacher. You (students) should check off each element when you are sure it is included in your paper. Turn in the checklist with each assignment to be used by your teacher for grading.

More advanced additions are in gray boxes on the checklist. You will see *vocabulary words* in this box. This is because you are encouraged to use some vocabulary words in each composition you write. Doing so will help you master these quality words. Your teacher will decide how to reward you for using them. She may also sometimes ask you to add another element of style she would like you to try. If she will assign point values to these, she will have you write the new total points possible on the custom total line.

Customizing the Checklist

The total point value of each assignment is indicated at the bottom of each checklist. This total reflects only the basic items, not the more advanced additions in the gray boxes. If these are used, add the appropriate amount of points, and write the new total on the custom total line.

Important: If students are not yet ready for a basic element on the checklist, simply have them cross it out. Subtract its point value from the total possible, and write the new total on the custom total line at the bottom.

If you would like to add elements to the checklist, assign each a point value, and add these points to the to the total possible, placing the new total on the custom total line. However, I like to make extra elements of style (e.g., vocabulary words and decorations) worth extra credit tickets instead (see Appendix 6). I find this to be more motivating to students than points toward their grades. I encourage all students to include vocabulary words.

Grading with the Checklist

To use the checklists for grading, do not try to add all the points earned. Instead, if an element is present, put a check in the blank or box next to it. If an element is missing, write the negative point value on its line or box. Total the negative points, and subtract them from the total points possible (or your custom total). *Hint: Use a different color of ink from the color the student used on the checklist.*

The Student Resource Notebook (SRN)

The *Student Resource Notebook* is a free download used throughout these lessons. Please follow the instructions on the blue page for downloading this very helpful resource at no cost. If you prefer not to print so many pages, you may purchase a hard copy from IEW.

Polished Draft Notebook

You should polish and illustrate each of your final drafts as soon as they have been checked and returned by a teacher. To do so, make all the corrections noted, and add a picture. This last draft is referred to as "the polished draft" and does not have to be labeled. Polished drafts should be kept in a binder in clear sheet protectors *with the original, labeled final draft hidden behind each.* At the end of the year, you will have a collection of a variety of types of compositions that move through major themes in medieval history.

See Appendix 2 for more details about this notebook.

In addition to the SRN,

encourage students to bring a thesaurus to class. Most kids enjoy using an electronic thesaurus, but for those who prefer books, IEW offers a unique one entitled *A Word Write Now*. A more traditional one that I like for elementary students is *The Clear and Simple Thesaurus and Dictionary* by Harriet Wittles and Joan Greisman. For older students, I highly recommend *The Synonym Finder* by J.I. Rodale. You can buy multiple copies of the latter two (used) very cheaply on the Internet and have them available in class.

This schedule is provided to emphasize to parents and students, particularly in a class setting, that students should not expect to complete an entire lesson in one day. Spreading the work throughout the week will produce much better writing with much less stress. Parents teaching their own children at home should follow a similar schedule.

Suggested Weekly Schedule

In general, lessons are designed to be taught weekly and to be completed as follows.

Day 1

1. Review concepts from previous lessons using activities in the Teacher's Manual.

2. Together, teacher and students read the new concept introduced in the lesson and do suggested activities. Then, follow Day 1 instructions to read the source text, make a key word outline, and tell back the meaning of the notes.

3. Use the brainstorming page to discuss ideas for including elements of style.

4. Discuss the vocabulary words for the present lesson.

5. Experienced IEW students who are ready for a more advanced assignment can be instructed to additionally do the extra source text in the *Medieval History-Based Advanced Writing Lessons Blackline Masters*, if there is one, or to add more advanced elements of style.

Days 2–3

1. Before returning to the new lesson, if work from a previous lesson has been returned with corrections to be made, polish this work with the help of a parent. Add a picture. Once checked, the polished draft will be placed in the polished draft notebook (see p. 6) with the original, labeled final draft behind it, in the same sheet protector. *Please see Appendix 2 for more details. There is a polished draft checklist on page 222.*

2. Cut out and learn the vocabulary words for the present lesson. Review previous.

3. Review the key word outline from Day 1 of the new lesson. If a note is unclear, check the source text, and add what you need to in order to understand it. *After you are sure you understand your notes*, use the outline and the brainstorming ideas to write or type a composition *in your own words*. Try not to look back at the source text while you are writing. Include and label everything on the checklist. Let an editor proofread.

Day 4

1. Review all vocabulary words learned thus far.

2. Write or type a final draft by making any corrections your editor asked you to make. (This will be fairly easy if the first draft was typed.) Check off each item on the checklist when you have included and labeled it.

3. Let an editor proofread again. He or she should check that all elements of structure and style are included and labeled as instructed on the checklist. Paperclip the checklist to your final draft to be turned in.

Labeling Dress-Ups

The lessons require one of each dress-up to be underlined in each paragraph. In addition, you may ask students to label each in the right margin using abbreviations (-ly, w-w, v, b/c, adj). Labeling will make grading simpler for teachers, and it will help students keep track of the elements to be sure that they use one of each.

Scope and Sequence

Lesson	Subject and Structure	Style (First Introduced)	Vocabulary	Literature Suggestions
Unit 1 1	Note Making and Outlines **The Middle Ages** Symbols and Abbreviations Advanced: Extra paragraph		fetid, massive, dilapidated, intrepid	
Unit 2 2	Writing from Notes **The Middle Ages**, continued Creating a Title	-ly Adverbs	stunned, flee, tenacious, desecrate	
3	**Anglo-Saxons** Advanced: King Arthur	*Who-which* clause	melancholy, imminent, bewildered, embellish	Lessons 3–6 *Beowulf* by Michael Morpurgo
4	**Beowulf** Advanced: Two paragraphs		resolved, brandish, spew, fatal	
5	**Byzantine Empire** Advanced: Constantinople	Proofreading Marks		
Unit 3 6	Retelling Narrative Stories **Augustine** Story Sequence Chart		extol, fatigued, rebuked, intrigued	
7	**Mohammed** Advanced: Extra paragraph	Strong Verbs	pursue, hastily, vacant, credible	Lessons 7–8 Tales from *1001 Arabian Nights*
8	**Ali and the Sultan's Saddle**	Alliteration	anguish, insolent, restrain, gravely	
9	**The Sword in the Stone**		disclosed, contrite, scowl, dislodge	Lessons 9–13 Chapters from *The Legend of King Arthur*
10	**Borrowing a Conflict** Advanced: Rhyming Story	Because clause		
Unit 4 11	Summarizing a Reference **Alfred the Great** Topic Sentence-Clincher Rule		prominent, myriad, virtue, endure	
12	**Charlemagne**, Part 1 Advanced: Extra topic	Similes	uniform, perturbed, foremost, reform	
13	**Charlemagne**, Part 2 2-or 3-Paragraph Structure		bestow, devout, renowned, proficient	
14	**Vikings** Advanced: Extra topic			Lessons 14–17 *The King's Shadow* by Elizabeth Alder
15	**A Year to Remember:** **The Battle of Hastings** Advanced: William the Conqueror		apprehend, stymied, plummet, interminable	
Unit 5 16	Writing from Pictures **The Magic Lamp**	Quality Adjectives Advanced: Duals	relish, abashed, ludicrous, capriciously	
17	**The King and the Dragon**	3sss Advanced: Triple extensions	din, crane, reprehensible, repugnant	

Institute for Excellence in Writing

Scope and Sequence

Lesson	Subject and Structure	Style (First Introduced)	Vocabulary	Literature Suggestions
Unit 6 18	Summarizing Multiple References **Medieval Cathedrals** Fused Outlines	www.asia clause	grandiose, serene, toil, contrive	Lessons 18–19 *Otto of the Silver Hand* by Howard Pyle
19	**Knights**, Part 1		feeble, clad, scorn, elite	
20	**Knights**, Part 2	#2 sentence opener	agile, impeccable, smug, indolent	Lessons 20–23 *Robin Hood* by J. Walker McSpadden (or children's version)
21 Library Research	**King Richard and His Brother John**			
Unit 7 22	Inventive Writing **Favorite Amusements**, Part 1	#3 sentence opener		
23	**Favorite Amusements**, Part 2	anecdotal opener		
24	**Twenty-First-Century Descriptive Letter**	#4 sentence opener		Lesson 24 *Marco Polo* by Demi
Unit 8 25	Formal Essay Models **Knights**, Part 3	Dramatic open-close: vss		Lessons 24–27 *The Kite Rider* by Geraldine McCaughrean
Unit 9 26	Formal Critiques **"Genghis Khan and His Hawk"**	Advanced: Avoid "you"	analyze, aghast, tragic, rash	
27	Response to Literature **"The Determined Samurai"**	#5 sentence opener		
Unit 8 w/Library Research 28	**Renaissance Men: da Vinci and Michelangelo (or men of choice)** Advanced: Alternate topic			Lessons 28–31 *Crispin: The Cross of Lead* by Avi
29	**Renaissance Men: Raphael (or choice)** Advanced: Alternate topic			
30	**Renaissance Men:** Introduction, Conclusion, Bibliography			
Just for Fun 31	**Vocabulary Story**		Review all	

Adapting the Schedule and Lessons

Adapting the Schedule and Lessons

These medieval lessons provide several assignments for practicing each of the IEW units. Most lessons are intended to be taught in one week. However, be aware that Lessons 9 and 26 are fairly lengthy, so younger students may need to spend two weeks on these. If you have fewer than the necessary weeks in your school calendar, you may omit a lesson or two from each unit without disrupting the flow of teaching the writing skills. The following chart suggests which lessons to omit and things to be aware of if you do.

First-Year Students (for a 24- to 25-Week Schedule)

Unit	Lesson	Title	Notes
2	5	The Byzantine Empire	
3	8	"Ali and the Sultan's Saddle"	Teach alliteration with Lesson 9. Assign Lesson 8 vocabulary with Lesson 9.
3	10	Borrowing a Conflict	
4	14	Vikings	Take Vocabulary Quiz 3 with Lesson 15. Also, remember to suggest the optional reading, *The King's Shadow*. (It's a must read!)
6	21	King Richard and His Brother John	
	31	Vocabulary Story	

You might also consider teaching Lessons 1 and 2 together.

Adapting for Experienced Level B Students

The optional advanced lessons in the *Medieval History-Based Advanced Writing Lessons Blackline Masters* (see the blue page) contain more advanced source texts. In addition, some pages suggest introducing more advanced elements of structure or style to students who are already comfortable with the basic requirements on the checklists. After they complete the regular lesson, feel free to use these extra helps to keep your veteran students progressing.

Teachers, review Unit 1: Note Making and Outlines in the TWSS workbook before teaching Lesson 1. If you have the seminar on DVD, watch the corresponding lesson.

Then, to teach the lesson, read through it with your students, and follow the assignment instructions for Day 1 in class. Go over instructions for Days 2–4, to be completed during the remainder of the week.

Unit 1: Note Making and Outlines

Lesson 1: The Middle Ages

In this book you will learn many ways to make your writing more exciting and more enjoyable to read. You will learn to write with structure and with style.

Structure

What is *structure*? Structure, in terms of writing, is basically how the ideas in a composition are organized. But when we simply say the word *structure*, often a building comes to mind. That is because buildings have many parts that need to be put together in a well-organized manner. They have structure.

Think of a castle. What had to happen before it was built? Someone had to draw out the plans for the builders to follow. The builders had to follow the plans so that each part was in its proper place. The royal family certainly would not have wanted the moat placed around their thrones or a torture chamber in their bedroom. Each part had to be placed in its own special spot, and each step had to be completed in its proper order.

Writing a paper is much the same. If we were just to begin writing without planning, our facts and details would probably not be arranged in the most logical way. Our composition would not be structured well and would not communicate our thoughts effectively. So in this course, you will "draw plans" for everything before you write. Your "plans" will be outlines, and they will follow a particular model for each type of composition.

Style

What comes to your mind when you hear the word *style*? Many people think of clothes. Clothes come in a variety of styles. A maiden would dress differently to go to a royal ball than she would to tend to her garden. That is because formal events require a formal style of clothing, whereas casual settings do not.

There are also different styles of language. Below are two sentences that communicate the same information in different styles. Which do you like better? Why?

> *He fell!*
>
> *The young knight plummeted headlong from his horse, dashing his hopes of winning the fair princess.*

You probably like the second better because it is more descriptive. However, what if you were at the joust with your friend and the knight was your brother. Which of the two sentences would be better for you to say? Obviously, the first would be more appropriate. Why the difference?

When you are speaking to people, they are there with you, experiencing the same scene and event as you are. You do not need to fill in the details. When you write, however, you must realize that the readers are not with you and cannot see, hear, or feel what is in your mind. You must help them see, hear, feel, and experience the scene you are writing about. IEW's elements of style will help you do this.

Key Word Outlines

Before you begin to write, you will practice the first step of learning structure in writing: key word outlining.

Structure is how you organize the things you write. Key word outlining will help you gather information and organize that information in your compositions.

When you outline, you will want to use or create some symbols or abbreviations to help you write quickly. You will find a list of commonly accepted symbols in the *Student Resource Notebook*. Below are a few symbols that we could use today. Some are from the SRN. Others are made up. What do you think each means?

b/c	☉	⊘	ppl	<u>XX</u>	→
because	time	no, not	people	died, dead	leads to; away

Practice key word outlining by following the assignment instructions on the following page.

Follow Day 1 instructions together. Read over Days 2–4, so students know how to complete the lesson during the week.

The Assignment

Day 1

1. Read the paragraph on page 14. Then read it again. With your teacher, choose *no more than three key words* from each sentence that will best help you remember the meaning of the sentence. Write the words on the blank outline on page 15.

   Note: You may use symbols, abbreviations, and pictures freely. They do not count as words. However, be sure you will remember what they mean.

Teachers, write class ideas on the whiteboard. Students may copy these or use their own ideas. See Sample KWO, page 15, for help.

2. Cover the source text and tell the meaning of each line of notes.

In a class, students should take turns, each telling the meaning of one line in a complete sentence.

3. Look at the vocabulary words for Lesson 1: *fetid, massive, dilapidated, intrepid.*

Have students turn to the vocabulary cards in the back of their books. Look at the words (picture side) for Lesson 1. Teachers can read a definition from the chart on page 260 and have students guess which word most likely matches it, using the pictures to help. Ask: *Could any be used in the paragraph we outlined?*

Day 2

1. Reread the paragraph on page 14; then, turn the page so you cannot see it. Using only your key word notes on page 15, try to tell back the information in complete sentences *in your own words*. You should not memorize the source text word for word. Rather, you should let the key words remind you of the key ideas. Then, state the ideas in your own words.

2. Cut out and learn the vocabulary words for Lesson 1 from Appendix 5. Put them in a pencil pouch where you can easily retrieve them when writing or studying for a quiz.

3. Try to add a vocabulary word to the outline of the Middle Ages paragraph(s).

Days 3–4

1. Prepare to give an oral report from your key word outline. Practice telling back the information, one line at a time. Look at a line; then look up and talk about it. Then look down at the next line, and look up and talk about it. Continue through the entire outline this way. Practice until the paragraph is smooth.

2. Review the vocabulary words.

Option for experienced Level B students: Complete the lesson in your Student Book first. If your parent-teacher assigns it, you can do the same with the extra paragraph in the *Medieval History-Based Advanced Writing Lessons Blackline Masters.*

Unit 1: Note Making and Outlines

Source Text

The Middle Ages

The Middle Ages is often thought of as a magnificent time of knights, kings, and castles. However, it was not a glorious time for Europe. There, the Middle Ages began with the crumbling of the Western Roman Empire in the late 400s. Different tribes of warriors stormed across Europe and seized parts of it. These barbarians had no interest in the arts or in learning, so this time is often called the Dark Ages. Knights and castles did not appear until late in the Middle Ages, around the 900s. Even then, most people were poor peasants who worked from sunup to sundown farming for the few noblemen. Life in the Middle Ages was filled with hardships, so education and the glorious Roman culture were almost forgotten.

Key Word Outline - "The Middle Ages"

I. _____ *M-A, thot, knights, castles* _____

   1. _____ *⊘, glorious, Europe* _____

   2. _____ *began, w/↓ , W. Rom. Emp., 400s* _____

   3. _____ *warriors, stormed, seized* _____

   4. _____ *⊘ like, arts, ed, "Dark Ages"* _____

   5. _____ *knights, castles, late (900s)* _____

   6. _____ *most, ppl, poor, farm* _____

   7. _____ *life, hard, Rom, cult, forgotten* _____

Unit 1: Note Making and Outlines

Teachers, review Unit 2: Writing from Notes in the *TWSS Seminar Workbook* before teaching Lessons 2–5. If you have the seminar on DVD, watch the corresponding lesson.

Unit 2: Writing from Notes

Lesson 2: The Middle Ages, continued

Review

1. Play Hangman.

See TM page 276. Use the phrase "partly ruined, broken down." Once solved, ask which vocabulary word this is. (dilapidated)

---

2. Share your oral report from Lesson 1.

Last week we focused on structure by learning to make key word outlines. This lesson will introduce you to the first element of style you will be required to use. IEW has three kinds of elements of style: dress-ups, decorations, and sentence openers. We will learn some of the dress-ups first. These are descriptive words or phrases that you can use to "dress-up" your writing.

-ly Adverbs

In this lesson we will have fun practicing the first dress-up: an -ly adverb.

An -ly adverb is simply a word that ends in an -ly. These words often tell how something happens. Can you think of any such words? If you have trouble, you can turn to the -ly adverbs section in the *Student Resource Notebook*. These pages give you a long list of just a few of the many -ly adverbs. Can you use some in sentences?

Have students turn to the -ly adverbs section in the SRN and create some sentences that contain -ly adverbs

---

Playing with -ly Adverbs

Choose different -ly adverbs to plug into the sentences below, and notice how the meaning of the scene is changed. You may use the -ly adverbs in the box below, those in the SRN, or -ly adverbs you think of on your own.

Here are two very different examples. Read the dialogue with only the first word in each blank. Then read it again with only the second word. Note how the scene drastically changes.

---

1. The king walked ___*happily angrily*___ to his throne room. There, a young knight was waiting for him.

   "What do you want?" he asked ___*eagerly hatefully*___.

   "Her," the knight replied ___*humbly evilly*___.

   "Me?" the princess gasped ___*sweetly woefully*___.

angrily	excitedly	humbly	longingly	smugly
anxiously	fearfully	hysterically	nervously	stubbornly
boldly	happily	innocently	rudely	suspiciously
eagerly	hatefully	intrepidly	savagely	sweetly
evilly	hopefully	joyfully	sheepishly	woefully

Break students into small groups. Have each group fill in the blanks. When all are done, have them read what they did. Compare and note how the different choices changed the feel of the scene.

Writing from Notes

In Lesson 1 you wrote a key word outline from a paragraph about the Middle Ages. Since you used this outline to give an oral report, you should be very familiar with the information. So in this lesson, you will learn to use the key word outline as a guide to write a paragraph. You will also practice adding the dress-up you have learned: the -ly adverb. Follow the steps below.

The Assignment

Day 1

1. Before you begin writing a paragraph, use page 19 to brainstorm ideas with your teacher for including -ly adverbs.

2. Using your key word outline of "The Middle Ages" as a guide, with your teacher's help, begin to write a paragraph *in your own words*. As you write, try to include some of the ideas for -ly adverbs from your brainstorming. Also, try to include one or more vocabulary words from Lessons 1 or 2.

   Put these in bold, or write *voc* in the right margin across from each.

Model the process of converting the KWO into a paragraph. Write student ideas on the whiteboard for the first few lines so that you know they have the idea. Include at least one -ly adverb and one vocabulary word. Offer an incentive for students to include vocabulary words in their paragraphs when they continue them. (I give a ticket for each. See Appendix 6.)

Here is a sample for the first few lines:

When people think of the Middle Ages, most often they <u>probably</u> think of **intrepid** knights, powerful kings, and massive castles. But medieval Europe was not so glorious. When the Middle Ages began in the 400s, the Western Roman Empire was **dilapidated**.

3. Go to page 20 to learn how to create a title for your work.

4. Go over the checklist on page 21. As you write your paragraph, put a ✔ in the box or blank for the requirements when you have done them. Note that you will need to underline one -ly adverb and bold or label vocabulary words. (Vocabulary words are not required, but you should try to use at least one.)

5. Look at the vocabulary words for Lesson 2: *stunned, flee, desecrate, tenacious.*

Days 2–4

1. Finish writing your paragraph using your key word outline, your brainstorming ideas, and the checklist to guide you. Check off each item on the checklist when you are sure it is completed. You will turn in the checklist with your paragraph.

2. Cut out the vocabulary words for Lesson 2. Learn them this week. Review the vocabulary words for Lessons 1 and 2. Try to include some in your paragraph(s).

Option for experienced students: Complete the lesson in your Student Book first. If your parent-teacher assigns it, you can do the same with the extra paragraph. See the *Medieval History-Based Advanced Writing Lessons Blackline Masters.*

Brainstorming Elements of Style

-ly Adverbs

List -ly adverbs that could fit in each of the blanks. Use the SRN -ly adverbs section for help.

1. *Sadly, Unfortunately, Eventually,* the Middle Ages brought the end of the

    glorious Roman culture in Europe.

2. Warriors charged *wildly, fearlessly* across Europe and

    savagely, greedily, brutally seized and desecrated parts of it.

3. Serfs worked *laboriously, miserably, constantly, tirelessly* , farming for their lords.

    Other ideas: _____

Vocabulary Ideas

Use at least two vocabulary words from Lessons 1 and 2 in sentences that could work in one of the Middle Ages paragraphs.

*The **massive** Roman Empire fell.*

*Great structures were **dilapidated**.*

***Intrepid** barbarians **desecrated** Roman cities.*

_____

_____

_____

Creating a Title

After you write your report, you must give it a creative title. Do not call it "The Middle Ages." Instead, try to repeat or reflect some of the key words from your title in your last sentence. This will help tie your report together. For example, the last sentence of the source text was this:

Life in the *Middle Ages* was *filled* with *hardships*, so *education* and the *glorious Roman*

culture were *almost forgotten.*

The italicized words above are the key words. Using these words or words that mean the same thing, more creative titles than "The Middle Ages" could be the following:

- "A Hard Life"

- "Forgotten Culture"

- "Faded Glory"

Can you think of other possibilities?

_____

_____

_____

(A Lost Culture; Almost Forgotten)

Go over each requirement with students. Explain that the gray box is for more advanced additions, which will usually include vocabulary words. Explain either how many points each is worth or what type of extra credit (or tickets) you will give for including these.

When grading, put a check mark in the box or line for each item that is completed correctly. Write the negative point value of items not completed correctly. Subtract the negative points from the total.

Lesson 2: The Middle Ages, continued

Lesson 2 Checklist - The Middle Ages, continued

FORMAT

☐ Name and date in upper left-hand corner _____ (5 pts)

☐ Composition double-spaced _____ (5 pts)

STRUCTURE

☐ Title repeats or reflects key words of last sentence. _____ (5 pts)

STYLE Each paragraph must contain at least one of each element of style.

Dress-Up (Underline one of each; abbreviate in right margin.)   (5 pts each)

☐ -ly adverb _____ (5 pts)

MORE ADVANCED ADDITIONS

☐ vocabulary words (Label voc or bold.) _____

☐ advanced paragraph- The Middle Ages around the World _____

Total _____/20

Custom total _____ / _____

Unit 2: Writing from Notes

Unit 2: Writing from Notes

Lesson 3: Anglo-Saxons

Review

Play Hangman.

Use these phrases: "title from last sentence" (When solved, ask student to explain.)

"not giving up or determined" (When solved, asked which vocabulary word? *tenacious*)

1. When writing a key word outline, how many words may you write from each sentence? What can you use freely?

three; symbols, abbreviations, pictures

2. How did you create your title? Share your title with the class.

by repeating or reflecting key words from the last sentence

In this lesson you will practice writing from a key word outline again, and you will learn another IEW dress-up.

The *Who-Which* Clause

In this lesson you will learn to add another dress-up to your paragraphs: a *who-which clause*. A *who* or *which* clause (*w-w clause*) is a clause that begins with either the word *who* or the word *which* and tells more information about a person, place, or thing.

A *who* clause will tell more about a person.

A *which* clause will tell more about a thing.

> Serfs, <u>who</u> served their lords, did not own the land they farmed.
>
> Castles, <u>which</u> were stone fortresses, protected a king and his nobles.

Notice that each of the *who-which* clauses has a comma before and after it. That is because it is inserted into a sentence that was already complete. You could take it out of the sentence and still have a complete sentence left. Try it and see.

Read each sentence above without the *who-which* clause.

Warning

You cannot just insert the word *who* or the word *which* into a sentence to make a *who-which* clause. If you do, you will create a fragment. For example, if you begin with *barbarians invaded Europe*, and simply add the word *who*, notice what you have:

Barbarians, who invaded Europe

This is a fragment. You must now add more information to make a complete sentence:

Barbarians, <u>who</u> invaded Europe, caused the crumbling of the Roman Empire.

Indicate a *who-which* clause by underlining the *who* or the *which*. Be sure that if the clause is removed, you still have a complete sentence left.

Practice

Add *who* or *which* clauses to the sentences below. Remember to place commas before and after each clause. Underline the *who* or the *which*.

1. Fire-breathing dragons, __*which* terrorized the land__ , are common in medieval tales.

2. Knights, __*who* fought intrepidly__ , often saved the town from these beasts.

Note: Use *which* for animals unless they are characters in stories and are acting like people, e.g., talking.

The Assignment

Day 1

1. Read the source text on page 26. With your teacher, make a key word outline.

2. Cover the source text, and tell the meaning of each line of notes.

3. Before you write a paragraph from your notes, use page 28 to brainstorm ideas for including a *who* or *which* clause and -ly adverbs.

4. Note the vocabulary words for Lesson 3: *melancholy, imminent, bewildered, embellish.* Discuss how to add some vocabulary words.

5. Turn to Appendix 1: Modified MLA Format. Notice how to format your paper.

Days 2–4

Follow the suggested schedule on page 7:

Students do not have anything to polish yet.

1. During the remainder of the week, write your own paragraph using your key word outline and your brainstorming ideas to guide you.

2. Include and underline the elements of style on the checklist on page 29 (-ly adverb and w-w clause). Check off each item when you are sure you have completed it.

3. Attach the checklist to your final draft.

Literature Suggestion

With Lessons 3–6 read *Beowulf* by Michael Morpurgo (see Appendix 4).

Option for experienced students: See the *Medieval History-Based Advanced Writing Lessons Blackline Masters* to follow the same procedure to add a second paragraph about King Arthur.

Unit 2: Writing from Notes

Source Text

The Anglo-Saxons

When the Western Roman Empire fell, Anglo-Saxon tribes from northern Europe crossed the North Sea. They wanted better land, so they invaded Britain. The Angles settled the southern part of the island. They called it *Angleland*, which evolved into *England*. The Angles gave us the English language. The Anglo-Saxons also brought their pagan religion to the land. The name of the king of their gods, Woden, gave us the English word for Wednesday (Woden's day). But in 598, a monk named Augustine traveled to England. He preached to the Angles, and many of them were converted to Christianity. The Anglo-Saxons ruled England proudly until 1066.

Key Word Outline - "Anglo-Saxons"

I. _____ W. Rom. Emp., ⬇, Anglo-Sax, ➔ N. Sea _____

1. _____ invaded, Britain _____

2. _____ Angles, settled, S _____

3. _____ called, Angleland, ➔ England _____

4. _____ gave, Eng, land _____

5. _____ A-S, brought, pagan, rel _____

6. _____ god, Woden, ➔ Wednes. (Woden's Day) _____

7. _____ AD 598, monk, Augustine, ➔ Eng _____

8. _____ > A-S, converted _____

9. _____ A-S, ruled, til, 1066 _____

Unit 2: Writing from Notes

Brainstorming Elements of Style

Who-Which Clauses

Combine each pair of sentences by using a *who* or *which* clause. Underline the *who* or the *which* because that is how you will indicate them in your compositions. To test, cover your w-w clause, and be sure there is still a complete thought left.

Hint: Be sure to put the who-which clause directly after the person or thing it describes.

1. The Angles settled in Britain. They wanted better land.

   The Angles, who wanted better land, settled in Britain.

2. Woden was an Anglo-Saxon god. His name gave us our word Wednesday.

   Woden, who was an Anglo-Saxon god, gave us our word Wednesday.
   Another possibility: Woden, who gave us our word for Wednesday, was an Anglo-Saxon god.

Add more detail to the following sentence using a *who-which* clause:

3. Augustine preached to the Angles.

   Two possibilities: 1. Augustine, who was a Catholic monk, preached to the Angles.

   2. Augustine preached to the Angles, who were pagans.

Ideas for -ly Adverbs

Augustine preached

   boldly, lovingly, intrepidly, tenaciously

Other Ideas

_____

_____

_____

Lesson 3 Checklist - Anglo-Saxons

FORMAT

☐ Modified MLA format (see Appendix 1)   _____ (5 pts)

STRUCTURE

☐ Title repeats or reflects key words from last sentence.   _____ (5 pts)

STYLE Each paragraph must contain at least one of each element of style.

Dress-Ups (Underline one of each; abbreviate in right margin.)   **(5 pts each)**

☐ -ly adverb   _____ (5 pts)

☐ *who-which* clause   _____ (5 pts)

MORE ADVANCED ADDITIONS

☐ vocabulary words (*Label voc or bold.*)   _____

☐ advanced paragraph- King Arthur   _____

Total _____ /20

Custom total _____ / _____

Unit 2: Writing from Notes

Institute for Excellence in Writing

Unit 2: Writing from Notes

Lesson 4: Beowulf

If you are returning work from Lesson 2, explain corrections as necessary. Students should polish their work and add pictures. The same should be done anytime a final draft is returned.

See Appendix 2 for more explanation of polished drafts.

Review

1. Go over vocabulary words for Lesson 4: *resolved, brandish, spew, fatal*; then play a vocabulary game from the Teacher's Manual, Appendix 6.

Around the World or Elimination would be good choices. You may need to repeat the same sixteen words several times, but that is great for review.

2. Read a *who-which* clause from your Anglo-Saxon paragraph.

The Assignment

Day 1

1. Read "Beowulf's Last Battle," on page 32. Make a KWO.
2. Cover the source text, and tell the meaning of each line of notes.
3. With your class, complete the brainstorming on page 34.
4. Look at the vocabulary words for Lesson 4: *resolved, brandish, spew, fatal*.

Days 2–4

Follow the suggested schedule on page 7:

1. Polish "The Middle Ages" paragraph from Lesson 2. Please See Appendix 2 for how to do this.

Teachers, take time to explain carefully how you would like your students to polish and turn in polished drafts. I have my students turn them in inside sheet protectors, with the original final draft hidden behind the first page and the polished draft checklist (half of page 222) in front of the first page. That way, when I give them back, they are ready to place in their polished draft notebook.

2. Write the story of Beowulf's Last Battle *in your own words*, using your key word outline and your brainstorming ideas to guide you. Do not look back at the source text.
3. Include and label everything on the checklist on page 35. Check off each item when you are sure you have completed it.
4. Attach the checklist to your final draft.

> ***Important:*** Study for *Vocabulary Quiz 1*. It will cover words from Lessons 1–4.

Options for experienced students: *The Medieval History-Based Advanced Writing Lessons Blackline Masters* provide a 2-paragraph, more detailed source text for this story.

Background

One of the oldest literary works written in the old English of the Anglo-Saxons is a long poem called Beowulf. The story is about a warrior, Beowulf, who sails to Denmark to fight a monster named Grendel. He defeats this monster as well as the monster's angry mother. He soon becomes king of the land and rules for many, many years. Here is a simplified version of the end of the story.

Source Text

Beowulf's Last Battle

Deep in a cave high on a cliff above the sea, a fierce dragon slept, guarding a vast treasure. One day a runaway slave found the cave and took a gorgeous golden goblet. The angry monster darted from village to village, spewing fire from his nostrils. The king, Beowulf, knew he must stop the beast from terrorizing the villages. He called to the monster, and the sinister serpent roared and hissed as the ground quaked with his steps. Beowulf and the dragon fought fiercely. Beowulf's sword broke, and the dragon seized him by the neck. A youngster climbed on the monster and stabbed at his throat until he finally dropped the king. Then the two stabbed at the beast until he died. The town was safe, but Beowulf had been fatally wounded.

Key Word Outline - "Beowulf's Last Battle"

I. _____ *cave,* ⬆ *cliff, dragon, treas* _____

1. _____ *slave, gold, goblet* _____

2. _____ ➔ *dragon, fire, villages* _____

3. _____ *Beowulf, must, stop* _____

4. _____ *called, monster, roared* _____

5. _____ *2 fought* _____

6. _____ *B's (draw sword), broke, dragon, neck* _____

7. _____ *youngster,* ⬆*, stabbed, dropped, B* _____

8. _____ *B + young, XX, beast* _____

9. _____ *town, safe, B, XX* _____

Unit 2: Writing from Notes

Brainstorming Elements of Style

Who-Which Clauses and -ly Adverbs

Finish each sentence. Include both a *who* clause and an -ly adverb. Remember the comma after the clause. Remember to finish the sentence after the clause.

1. The dragon, <u>who</u> *was angry, mercilessly charred the villages* .

2. Beowulf, <u>who</u> *had fought bravely, saved the land* .

Encourage the use of a thesaurus.

Vocabulary Ideas

Write phrases that could be in your story. Include vocabulary words.

the **massive** dragon's **fetid** breath

the **dilapidated** town

The **intrepid** youth did not **flee** but fought **tenaciously** for his king.

Beowulf's wound was **fatal**, so his death was **imminent**.

Institute for Excellence in Writing

Lesson 4 Checklist - Beowulf

FORMAT

☐ Modified MLA format (see Appendix 1)   _____ (5 pts)

STRUCTURE

☐ Title repeats or reflects key words from last sentence.   _____ (5 pts)

STYLE Each paragraph must contain at least one of each element of style.

Dress-Ups (Underline one of each; abbreviate in right margin.)   **(5 pts each)**

☐ -ly adverb   _____ (5 pts)

☐ *who–which* clause   _____ (5 pts)

MORE ADVANCED ADDITIONS

☐ vocabulary words (*Label voc or bold.*)   _____

☐ advanced paragraph- Beowulf's Last Battle   _____

Total _____ /20

Custom total _____ / _____

Unit 2: Writing from Notes

Unit 2: Writing from Notes

Lesson 5: The Byzantine Empire

Lesson 5: The Byzantine Empire

Take Vocabulary Quiz 1.

If you are returning work from Lesson 3, explain corrections as necessary. Kids should polish their work and add a picture. Do this anytime a final draft is returned. See Appendix 2 for more explanation of polished drafts.

Proofreading Marks

The SRN contains a list of common proofreading marks. Your teacher may have made some of these marks on the papers that were returned to you. Be sure you understand what each of the marks means. Use some of the marks to correct the errors in the following sentences:

The angles invaded the southern part of Britain. The land, which was called Angleand.

There language was the start of the English language the word Wednesday came from their

god, Woden.

Write the sentences on the whiteboard. With a different color of marker, show the proofreading marks you would use to correct the errors.

Three lines under the a in angles; "frag" after *called Angleland*; sp above *There*; RO between

     RO

English language ∧ and *the word Wednesday; slash through the capital G in God.*

The Assignment

Day 1

1. Read "The Byzantine Empire," on page 38. Make a KWO. Cover the source text and tell the meaning of each line of notes.

2. With your class, complete the brainstorming page, page 40.

3. There are no new vocabulary words for Lesson 5.

Days 2–4

Follow the suggested schedule on page 7.

1. Polish "The Anglo-Saxons" paragraph from Lesson 3. Please see Appendix 2 for how to do this.

2. Write the Byzantine Empire paragraph *in your own words*, using your key word outline. Include and label everything on the checklist. Check off each item when you are sure you have completed it. Attach the checklist to your final draft.

3. There are no new vocabulary words for Lesson 5.

Option for experienced students: In order to add a second paragraph about Constantinople, go to the *Medieval History-Based Advanced Writing Lessons Blackline Masters*, and follow the same procedure.

Unit 2: Writing from Notes

Source Text

The Byzantine Empire

While the Western Roman Empire fell to barbarians, some parts of the Eastern Roman Empire withstood attacks. This was the Byzantine Empire. The people there held on to the land around their capital city of Constantinople. Then, in 527, an emperor named Justinian the Great rose to power. He wanted to restore the greatness of the old Roman Empire, so his armies fought and recaptured some of the land that had been seized. He gathered and bound Roman laws into what has been called the Justinian Code. This code made laws all around his kingdom the same. His empire flourished, and Constantinople became the grandest city in the world.

Key Word Outline - "The Byzantine Empire"

I. _____ W. Rom. Emp ⬇, barbs, E. Rom Emp. ∅ _____

    1. _____ E = Byzantine Emp _____

    2. _____ ppl, held, cap, Constantinople _____

    3. _____ 527, emp, Justinian Great ⬆ _____

    4. _____ restore, > Rom Emp, recap, lands _____

    5. _____ gathered, laws, Justinian Code _____

    6. _____ = laws, same, everywhere _____

    7. _____ emp. ☺, Constantinople, > city _____

Brainstorming Elements of Style

-ly Adverbs

List -ly adverbs to describe the following ideas in your paragraph. Use the -ly adverb lists in the SRN for help.

1. How did the Eastern Roman Empire withstand attacks?

   triumphantly, bravely, tenaciously, mightily, successfully

2. How did Justinian's army fight and recapture some land?

   strategically, determinedly, successfully, valiantly, purposefully

3. How did Justinian gather and bind Roman laws?

   carefully, diligently, effectively, tirelessly, earnestly

Who-Which Clauses

Write a sentence that you could use in your paragraph that includes a *who-which* clause.

The Eastern Roman Empire, <u>which</u> was called the Byzantine Empire, remained strong.

Justinian the Great, <u>who</u> wanted to restore the great Roman culture, gathered its laws.

Vocabulary Words

Write some ideas for including some vocabulary words in your paragraph.

*The people of Constantinople fought tenaciously and **intrepidly** and did not **flee**.*

*While the **massive** Western Roman Empire became **dilapidated**, the Byzantine Empire*

*would not be **desecrated**.*

*Justinian was **resolved** to make his empire great.*

*Barbarian attacks proved **fatal** for the Western Roman Empire.*

Offer a ticket for each vocabulary word students can use in a sentence that could be part of this summary. They should look at their vocabulary chart in Appendix 5 for help.

Lesson 5 Checklist - The Byzantine Empire

FORMAT

☐ Modified MLA format (see Appendix 1)   _____ (5 pts)

STRUCTURE

☐ Title repeats or reflects key words from last sentence.   _____ (5 pts)

STYLE Each paragraph must contain at least one of each element of style.

Dress-Ups (Underline one of each; abbreviate in right margin.)   **(5 pts each)**

☐ -ly adverb   _____ (5 pts)

☐ *who-which* clause   _____ (5 pts)

MORE ADVANCED ADDITIONS

☐ vocabulary words (*Label voc or bold.*)   _____

☐ advanced paragraph- Constantinople   _____

Total _____ /20

Custom total _____ / _____

Unit 2: Writing from Notes

Teachers, review Unit 3: Retelling Narrative Stories in the TWSS workbook before teaching Lessons 6–10. If you have the seminar on DVD, watch the corresponding lesson.

If you are returning work from Lesson 4, first read some of the elements of style students did well. Also, explain corrections as necessary. Kids should polish their work and add a picture. The same should be done anytime a final draft is returned. See Appendix 2 for more explanation of polished drafts and the polished draft notebook.

Lesson 6: Augustine

Unit 3: Retelling Narrative Stories

Lesson 6: Augustine

Review

Play Vocabulary Lightning.

See TM, page 275.

The Story Sequence Chart

In this lesson you will learn to write stories. As in previous lessons, you will be provided with a source text from which to take notes; however, the note taking method will differ. You will use a note taking method that will help you appreciate the important elements of a story so that eventually you can use the technique to outline your own stories.

Every story, regardless of how long it is, contains the same basic elements:

Setting and Characters
Stories usually begin by introducing readers to the time and place of the story. This is called the *setting*. Descriptions of the setting often include descriptive words to help the readers see, hear, feel, smell, or taste things. We call these five-senses words. These kinds of words help readers feel as if they are there. They also help create the mood of the story. For example, a happy story might begin with blue skies, warm sunshine, and birds singing merrily, whereas a suspenseful story might begin with gray skies, howling wind, and rolling thunder.

Also at their beginnings, stories must introduce their readers to the main people (or animals) of the story: the *characters*.

Conflict and Plot
Then, for a story to be captivating, it must move into the next important element: the *conflict*. This is the problem, want, or need of the main character(s). Stories without some sort of problem to overcome, or need to be met, are not very interesting. Most of the action of the story is simply how the conflict is dealt with—what the characters do, say, think, or feel with respect to the conflict. This is known as the *plot*.

Climax and Resolution
If there is a conflict or problem, there must be a way to solve it! We call the event that leads to the problem being solved the *climax* of the story. It is often the most exciting part of the story. We call the result of the climax (how the problem works out) the *resolution*.

The characters and the readers should have learned something from the events of the story. This is the *message*, or theme. The message gives the story a sense of purpose. Without it, a reader may feel like there was no point to the story. However, the message is not usually stated.

Unit 3: Retelling Narrative Stories

The Assignment

Day 1

1. Read "The Archbishop of Canterbury" on the following page. With the help of your teacher, complete the outline by answering the Story Sequence Chart questions. Answer in key word notes.

   Your outline should be brief. You can add more details when you actually write your own version of story. Notes do not necessarily need to be placed on the line across from the questions they answer. For example, in Section I, it does not matter whether you introduce the setting or the characters first. You may also need more than one line to answer one question. You may be able to answer two questions on one line.

2. Take turns telling back the story, using one line of the outline at a time.

3. Begin to brainstorm ideas for elements of style on page 47.

4. Notice that the checklist requires one of each dress-up in each paragraph.

Teachers, be sure to go over the checklist with students. Show them the three columns. Be sure they understand that each is for one section of the story.

5. Look at the vocabulary words for Lesson 6: *extol, fatigued, rebuke, intrigued.*

Days 2–4

Follow the suggested schedule on page 7.

1. Polish the Beowulf story from Lesson 4.

2. Write your own version of the Augustine story, using your key word outline and brainstorming ideas. Do not look back at the source text. *Write in your own words. Add plenty of five-senses description.*

3. Include and label everything on the checklist. Each of the three sections of your story should have all dress-ups. Check off each item when you are sure you have completed it.

4. Attach the checklist to your final draft.

5. Cut out and learn the vocabulary words for Lesson 6. Review all. Try to use some in your story.

    Institute for Excellence in Writing

Option for experienced students: Consider encouraging your students to add more conversation to their stories. What would the pope say to the slave traders? What would Pope Gregory and Augustine say to each other when the pope summoned him and told him he wanted to send him to England? What would Augustine and the king say to each other?

The dominant religion in Western Europe during the Middle Ages was Roman Catholicism. One man, called the pope, was the supreme ruler. Under him were archbishops, who ruled large regions, bishops, who oversaw local churches, and monks, who lived in monasteries and devoted their lives to God and the church. The following story tells how Catholicism reached England, and how a monk became a great archbishop.

Source Text

The Archbishop of Canterbury

It was a cool, misty morning. As Pope Gregory walked through Rome, crowds of people pressed him toward the slave auction block. There, a strange sight caught his eye. At the slave market three boys looked different from any he had ever seen. Their hair and skin were almost pure white.

"Where did you find these boys?" he asked the slave traders.

"On the island of Britain," they said. "They are called Anglo-Saxons."

"I'll buy all three," the pope said as he reached for his money. "No one should have to be a slave."

Pope Gregory took the boys home with him and asked them about their land and their religion. He discovered that they knew nothing about the God of the Bible.

Pope Gregory became deeply saddened. He desired to send missionaries to England, so he sent for Augustine.

"Augustine," he said, "you must go to England and tell the people about the Lord."

Augustine agreed and sailed with a group of monks. As they reached the shore of Britain, they were met by the king of the southern part of the island.

"Who are you, and what is your purpose here?" he asked.

"We're Christians, here to tell your people about God," Augustine proclaimed.

The king was very kind to the group of missionaries. "You may live in Canterbury and preach to my people," he said.

Many Anglo-Saxons were converted. On Christmas Day of 597, Augustine baptized thousands. The pope sent more monks to help Augustine, and churches were built all over southern England. The pope made Augustine the Archbishop of Canterbury, and some people called him, "The Apostle of England."

Unit 3: Retelling Narrative Stories

The Story Sequence Chart

Setting, Characters, Background

What is the setting? Describe it. Who are the characters? Tell about them.	I. _____ M-A Rome, slave, market_ 1. _____ drizzly, loud, busy_ 2. _____ Pope Greg, ⊙ ⊙, 3 slaves_ 3. _____ boys, strange, white, A-S_ 4. _____ bought, "⊘ B slave," ➔ home_

Plot or Problem

What is the problem? What do the characters do, say, think, and feel? What happens before the climax?	II. _____ disc, A-S, ⊘ God, Bible_ 1. _____ ☹, sent 4, Augustine, missionary_ 2. _____ Aug, w/40 monk, ➔ Eng_ 3. _____ reached, S island_ 4. _____ ⊙ ⊙, king, "Who? Why?"_

Climax and Resolution

What leads to the conflict being solved (the climax)? What happens as a result?	III. _____ Aug, "Tell, ppl, God"_ 1. _____ 👑, "live, Canterbury, preach"_ 2. _____ >, A-S, converted, 1000s bapt, Christmas 597_ 3. _____ pope, ➔ ⬆ monks, churches_ 4. _____ Aug, Archbishop, Canterbury_

Institute for Excellence in Writing

Brainstorming Elements of Style

-ly Adverbs

List -ly adverbs to describe the following ideas in your paragraph:

1. How did the pope speak to the slave traders?
   (... the pope asked _____ or ... the pope stated _____)

   furiously, sternly, resolutely, calmly, crossly, frankly

2. How did the pope speak to the boys?
   (... the pope questioned _____ or ... the pope stated _____)

   kindly, curiously, sympathetically, intently, reassuringly, serenely, tenderly

3. How did the king respond to Augustine?
   (... the king answered _____)

   enthusiastically, gratefully, joyfully, generously, wholeheartedly

Who-Which **Clauses**

Write a sentence that you could use in your paragraph that includes a *who-which* clause.

Answers will vary. Check to be sure commas are used correctly and that students do not create fragments.

Here is one idea: Pope Gregory, <u>who</u> desired to send a missionary to England,

called for Augustine.

Vocabulary Words

Write some ideas for including some vocabulary words in your paragraph.

Have students turn to page 260. Offer a ticket for each word a student can use in a sentence that could be part of the story. Here are a few ideas:

The pope was <u>intrigued</u> and <u>bewildered</u> by the slave boys.
The pope <u>rebuked</u> the slave traders.
It was a <u>melancholy</u> day at the slave market, which was surrounded by
   <u>dilapidated</u>, <u>fetid</u> shacks.
The pope bargained <u>tenaciously</u> for the slaves, who looked <u>fatigued</u> after their
   long voyage to Rome.

Describing the Setting

Skilled writers try to describe the places of their stories in a way that the reader feels as if he is there. Using words that appeal to the five senses (see, hear, feel, smell, taste) can help accomplish this. Find the five-senses section in the SRN that lists such words. Which sense does each of the underlined words below appeal to?

> A _cool breeze_ lifted the _sweaty gray_ hair off Pope Gregory's forehead. The _bustling_
>
> streets of Rome _teemed_ with people this morning, so it was _warm_ under his cloak despite the
>
> _chilly_ air. Gulls _screeched loudly_ overhead. The auctioneer _rambled annoyingly_ on and on.
>
> Gregory looked up at the auction block.

Imagine that you are the pope walking down the streets of Rome. What is the day like? Consider things such as the following: Is it morning, afternoon, or evening? Is it warm or cold? Is the air clear, foggy, dreary, wet, or dry? Is it still or windy? Is the sky sunny, cloudy, blue, dusky orange, or gray?

Ask the above questions. Let each student write ideas to describe the day as he or she pictures it.

> What would you see, hear, or feel around you, especially as you near the slave auction? Describe each with five-senses words.

dusty, bumpy cobblestone streets winding; blue-green water in the distance with tall masts bobbing; grandiose marble buildings; crowds of people bustling; sad, dejected faces of slaves; dirty, muscular slave trader

people chattering or yelling; harsh bellowing of slave traders; clinking and clanking of chains; shuffle of feet; whimpers or wails of the slaves

thick, moist air; slick or dusty streets; muggy air

> Add such descriptions to your story, especially in the beginning, which should describe the setting.

It might be fun to allow students to work in pairs for this.

_____

_____

_____

_____

Lesson 6 Checklist - Augustine

FORMAT

☐ Modified MLA format (see Appendix 1)   _____ (5 pts)

STRUCTURE

☐ Title repeats or reflects key words from last sentence.   _____ (5 pts)

☐ Story Sequence Chart followed   _____ (5 pts)

STYLE Each section must contain at least one of each element of style.

¶ 1 ¶ 2 ¶ 3 Dress-Ups (Underline one of each; abbreviate in right margin.)   **(5 pts each)**

☐   ☐   ☐   -ly adverb   _____ (15 pts)

☐   ☐   ☐   *who–which* clause   _____ (15 pts)

Because dialogue requires paragraph breaks, each dress-up does not need to be in every paragraph, but in each of the three story sequence sections.

MORE ADVANCED ADDITIONS

☐ vocabulary words (*Label voc or bold.*)   _____

☐ conversation   _____

Total _____/45

Custom total _____ / _____

Unit 3: Retelling Narrative Stories

Unit 3: Retelling Narrative Stories

Lesson 7: Mohammed

Review

1. Play the five-senses game from the TM.

2. What is wrong with the following?

I often begin class by putting on the whiteboard samples of common grammar errors students made in previous assignments. We discuss the errors. It is a great way to review the grammar rules you desire your students to remember. This week, there are a couple of sample ideas below that reflect common errors in using quotation marks.

> *"You don't know about God of the Bible!" "He is the creator of the universe!"*
> *Exclaimed the pope.*

You do not need to end and begin the quotation marks between the first two sentences since the pope says both. Do not capitalize *exclaimed* because it is still part of the sentence with the quote.

> *"Augustine, said the pope, would you sail to Britain to tell the people about*
> *Jesus Christ"?*

Put an end quote mark after Augustine, (after the comma). Place beginning quote marks in front of *would*. Place the final end quote marks after the question mark.

Strong Verbs

In this lesson you will learn about *strong verbs*. Strong verbs are words that show *action*. They tell what someone or something is *doing*. However, some verbs that show action are boring and are not easy to picture. For example, *came* is a verb, but it is vague, as in the following sentence:

> *The princess came into the kitchen.*

Did she *storm* into the kitchen? Did she *tiptoe* into the kitchen? Did she *dance* into the kitchen? Did she *sneak* into the kitchen?

Storm, *tiptoe*, *dance*, and *sneak* are all much stronger verbs than *came*.

Using *strong verbs* will make your writing much more exciting.

We are going to ban some verbs because they are too boring. Here are the verbs that you may not use for this class.

Banned Verbs

go/went   say/said

The banned verbs are also listed in the beginning section of the SRN. Memorize which verbs are banned. There are substitutes for these verbs in the strong verbs section of the SRN. Tab that section.

Practice

In each sentence, cross out the banned verb(s). On the line below each, write strong verbs that could replace them. You may use the SRN for help.

1. The dragon went over the castle.

   <u>*swooped, darted, glided, swept*</u>

2. They heard a soldier say, "They did not go in there."

   <u>*shout, comment, observe, exclaim   sneak, wander, escape*</u>

3. The prince said, "Who ate my stew?"

   <u>*whined, demanded, bellowed, blasted, exclaimed*</u>

The Assignment

Day 1

1. Read "Mohammed" on the following page. Follow the same instructions as for Lesson 6 to make an outline of the story.

2. Take turns telling back the story, using one line of the outline at a time.

3. Begin to brainstorm ideas for elements of style on page 56.

4. Notice that the checklist requires one of each dress-up in each paragraph.

5. Note the vocabulary words for Lesson 7: *pursue, hastily, vacant, credible*. Which one is a strong verb? *Pursue* is a verb. (Don't let *hastily* fool you. It tells *how* something is done, not *what* is done. It modifies a verb, but it is not a verb. We could use it with pursue: He <u>hastily</u> <u>pursued</u> the suspect.)

Days 2–4

1. Polish the Byzantine Empire report from Lesson 5.

2. Write your own version of the Mohammed story, using your key word outline and brainstorming ideas. Do not look back at the source text.

3. Include and label everything on the checklist. Attach it to your final draft.

4. Cut out and learn the vocabulary words for Lesson 7. Review all. Try to use some in your story.

Option for experienced students: Use the *Medieval History-Based Advanced Lessons Blackline Masters* to add an introductory paragraph to your story.

Advanced students may also be encouraged to use strong verbs to show the emotion of the characters in the story. In other words, what would Mohammed do when he saw the angel that would show he was frightened and in awe? (He might <u>fall</u> on his face, <u>tremble</u>, <u>cower</u>, <u>gape</u>. His heart would <u>pound</u>. His knees might *knock*.)

Literature Suggestion

With Lessons 7–8, read selected tales from *1001 Nights* by Geraldine McCaughrean. A simpler version is *Arabian Nights* from the Classic Start series (Sterling Publishing Company).

Have students circle banned verbs they notice. They are highlighted for teachers.

Roman Catholicism was the dominant religion of Europe in the Middle Ages, but another religion began during this time—Islam. Islam is the religion of the Muslims. It is based on the claims of a man named Mohammed (also spelled Muhammed). After he died, his teachings were collected in a book called the Koran (Quran). Islam spread through the Middle East and across Africa as Mohammed's followers, led by a warrior and leader named Abu Bakr, conquered surrounding lands. Today Islam is a major world religion. This is the story Muslims tell about how Islam began.

Source Text

Mohammed

Mohammed did not like the busy city of Mecca. Sometimes he went to the desert to be alone.

One of these times, he claimed that he was in a dark, quiet cave when he heard strange music.

He looked up and saw an angel surrounded by light. Next to him was a scroll with words written

in fire. Mohammed had never learned to read, but he said somehow he understood the message.

He was to be Allah's messenger. Mohammed went home to tell his wife what had happened. She

encouraged him.

After that, he claimed to receive more revelations from the angel, who told him to preach

in the city. Some people listened, but others did not. He made many enemies.

One day while he and his best friend and follower Abu Bakr sat at dinner, soldiers began

banging on the door. Mohammed and his friend ran from the house and dashed into a nearby

cave. Soon the soldiers were at the cave's opening, so Mohammed and Abu Bakr sat still and

listened.

"Look, there's a spider web across the entrance, so they can't be in there, or they would

have broken it," they heard one soldier say. The soldiers went on, and Mohammed made the

journey to Medina safely where he had many followers to welcome him. This was the beginning

of Islam.

The Story Sequence Chart

Setting, Characters, Background

What is the setting?	I.	_Mecca, busy, dirty_
Describe it.	1.	_Mohammed, ☹, ➜ cave, alone_
Who are the characters?	2.	_☉ ☉, angel, scroll, (draw fire)_
Tell about them.	3.	_⊘ read, understood, Allah's, mess_
	4.	_➜ home, wife, encouraged_

Plot or Problem

What is the problem?	II.	_> revelations, told, preach_
What do the characters do, say, think, and feel?	1.	_many, enemies_
	2.	_soldiers, door_
What happens before the climax?	3.	_he + Abu Bakr ➜ cave_

Climax and Resolution

What leads to the conflict being solved (the climax)?	III.	_soldiers, ☉ ☉, spider, web_
	1.	_"⊘ inside," broken_
	2.	_soldiers, left_
What happens as a result?	3.	_Mo, Medina, preached, safely_
	4.	_Beginning, Islam_

Unit 3: Retelling Narrative Stories

Brainstorming Elements of Style

Strong Verbs

Write strong verbs that could replace each of the banned words below. Use the SRN for help. Can you also put -ly adverbs with some of the strong verbs?

1. He *went* to the desert to be alone.

   retreated, escaped, ambled, sauntered—frequently

2. Even though he could not read, he *said* he understood the message.

   insisted, claimed, believed, declared—confidently

3. He *went* home to tell his wife.

   rushed, hurried, stumbled, fled, darted—frantically

4. "The web would be broken if they entered the cave," they heard one soldier *say*.

   reason, whisper, decide, deduce—logically

Describing Settings

This is a story, so remember to use five-senses words to help your reader see, hear, feel, smell, and taste. Write five-senses words to tell about each of the following. Especially focus on verbs and -ly adverbs where possible.

Mecca: (What did Mohammed see, hear, or feel that bothered him?) *(merchants bickered)*

   camels spitting, beggars wailing, burly, sweaty men, noisy children

cave: *(cool cave calmed him)*

   dark, dank cave instantly flooded with dazzling light

angel's appearance or voice: *(bright figure towered majestically)*

   voice boomed, thundered, echoed

words of fire: *(crackled loudly)*

   sizzled and seared, blazed and burned brightly

Institute for Excellence in Writing

Lesson 7 Checklist - Mohammed

FORMAT

☐ Modified MLA format (See Appendix 1.) _____ (5 pts)

STRUCTURE

☐ Title repeats or reflects key words from last sentence. _____ (5 pts)

☐ Story Sequence Chart followed _____ (5 pts)

STYLE Each section must contain at least one of each element of style.

¶ 1	¶ 2	¶ 3	**Dress-Ups** (Underline one of each; abbreviate in right margin.)	**(5 pts each)**
☐	☐	☐	-ly adverb	_____ (15 pts)
☐	☐	☐	*who–which* clause	_____ (15 pts)
☐	☐	☐	strong verb	_____ (15 pts)

MECHANICS

☐ banned words: go/went say/said _____ (-1 pt)

MORE ADVANCED ADDITIONS

☐ vocabulary words (*Label voc or bold.*) _____

☐ conversation _____

☐ advanced paragraph- Background _____

Total _____/60

Custom total _____ / _____

Unit 3: Retelling Narrative Stories

If you are returning work from Lesson 6 (Augustine), read some of the elements of style students did well. Be sure everyone understands any corrections you may have noted.

Unit 3: Retelling Narrative Stories

Lesson 8: Ali and the Sultan's Saddle

Review
Play a quick vocabulary game from the TM.

Decorations
Stories are the perfect place to use some IEW decorations. Decorations are fancier than dress-ups and add much sophistication to stories.

Alliteration
In this course, *alliteration* is simply using three or more words close together that begin with the same sound. Our ear likes the repetition of sound like that. Which of the following sentences includes alliteration? Which do you like the sound of better?

1. The flattered Sultan listened quietly.

2. The smitten Sultan sat silently.

Tongue twisters are exaggerated alliterations. Here are some popular tongue twisters:

"Peter Piper picked a peck of pickled peppers …"

"She sells sea shells down by the seashore …"

"Betty Botta bought a bit of bitter butter …"

Tongue twisters are fun, but they are not what we want in our stories. Three or four words close together that begin with the same sound will produce the more sophisticated effect we desire. You will practice using alliteration in your story after you outline it, but see if you can spot some in the source text as you read it.

The Assignment
Follow the instructions from Lessons 6–7 to outline the new story in this lesson ("Ali and the Sultan's Saddle"). Then, use page 62 to brainstorm elements of style.

Remember to cut out and learn the new vocabulary words and polish the Augustine story.

Option for experienced students: See the *Medieval History-Based Advanced Writing Lessons Blackline Masters* to write and add Ali's poem to your story. What did he say about the sultan?

Veteran students who find alliteration easy may be encouraged to add similes as well, especially if they add Ali's poem. It is the perfect place to add similes because the story says he compares the sultan to the sun and to the mighty desert winds. See the *Seminar Workbook* for help with similes.

Source Text

Ali and the Sultan's Saddle
retold by Landen N. as "A Thrust and a Wink"

Once, in the far off Arabian desert in the midst of the burning plains of sand, there resided a kingdom. In this kingdom a palace stood tall in the center of the tremendous town. Now, the sultan* of this town happened to be very vain. A certain intrepid joker by the name of Ali, who liked to jab at the sultan's pride, went around the town telling hilarious yet insulting jokes about him from sunup to sundown. The townspeople, who evidently thought Ali was entertaining, eventually let word slip to the sultan.

Angry beyond words, the sultan demanded the presence of Ali. When Ali arrived at the palace, he bowed so low his head nearly touched the polished tile floor. Before the sultan could speak, Ali, obviously trying to delay the sultan, began to flatter him with admiring words. Impressed by the joker's soft words, the sultan attempted to stammer out his thanks to Ali. Again the swift joker did not let him speak. Instead, he asked the sultan if he might recite a poem he had made about the king. Though he had not really prepared any poem for the sultan, the quick-lipped Ali created one on the spot, comparing the Sultan to the sun and to the mighty desert winds. Everyone was intrigued.

The sultan was once again flattered. Ali made the king completely forget what he had summoned him for. Wanting to reward him, the sultan told Ali to choose a saddle from his storage. Picking out and strapping a rough, leathery donkey's saddle to his back, Ali the Joker rushed off to the center of town. Pausing in a populous plaza, Ali was asked by the townspeople where he had chanced upon the saddle.

"I visited the sultan," said the joker, "and he gave me one of his finest robes!" And with a wink and a thrust, he pointed to the saddle.

*_sultan_ is the title Muslims give to their rulers. It is derived from the Arabic word for strength, authority, power.

The Story Sequence Chart

Setting, Characters, Background

What is the setting? Describe it. Who are the characters? Tell about them.	I. _____ *Arabian desert, >kingdom* _____
	1. _____ *city, w. > palace* _____
	2. _____ *sultan, vain, foolish* _____
	3. _____ *Ali, joker, insolent* _____
	4. _____ *mocked, sul, laugh* _____

Plot or Problem

What is the problem? What do the characters do, say, think, and feel? What happens before the climax?	II. _____ *sultan, heard, angry* _____
	1. _____ *summoned, punish* _____
	2. _____ *Ali, flattered* _____
	3. _____ *poem, cp sun, wind* _____
	4. _____ *all, intrigued* _____

Climax and Resolution

What leads to the conflict being solved (the climax)? What happens as a result?	III. _____ *sultan, forgot, angry* _____
	1. _____ *rewards, Ali, saddle* _____
	2. _____ *chooses, donkey's* _____
	3. _____ *➔ town, ppl, ask* _____
	4. _____ *"sultan, finest, robe"* _____

Brainstorming Elements of Style

Strong Verbs

Write strong verbs that could replace each of the banned words below. Use the SRN for help. Can you also put -ly adverbs with some of the strong verbs?

1. Ali went around town telling jokes about the Sultan.

   sauntered, pranced, strolled—haughtily, mockingly

2. Ali went back to town with the saddle on his back.

   skipped happily, trudged, shuffled quickly, dashed triumphantly

3. Ali said, "The Sultan gave me his finest saddle."

   joked, laughed, exclaimed, pronounced, mocked—insolently, jokingly,
   discreetly, cleverly

Alliteration

Fill in the blanks to create some alliteration. *(Hint: Lists of -ly adverbs, quality adjectives, and strong verbs in the SRN may be helpful. Look for words that begin with s.)*

the _____ _____ sultan _____

solemn, sullen, sulky, senseless, smitten, surly, simpleminded, stunned, surprised, sour, stupefied, sleek

stewed, soon summoned, sat silently, smiled with satisfaction, screamed, sneered, shrieked, sighed sadly

Write other ideas for alliteration in other parts of the story:

jauntily joked and jeered; reverently and resonantly recited; wild, whooshing wind

_____

_____

_____

Institute for Excellence in Writing

Lesson 8 Checklist - Ali and the Sultan's Saddle

FORMAT

☐ Modified MLA format (See Appendix 1.) _____ (5 pts)

STRUCTURE

☐ Title repeats or reflects key words from last sentence. _____ (5 pts)

☐ Story Sequence Chart followed _____ (5 pts)

STYLE Each section must contain at least one of each element of style.

¶ 1 ¶ 2 ¶ 3	Dress-Ups (Underline one of each; abbreviate in right margin.)	(5 pts each)	
☐ ☐ ☐	-ly adverb	_____ (15 pts)	
☐ ☐ ☐	*who–which* clause	_____ (15 pts)	
☐ ☐ ☐	strong verb	_____ (15 pts)	

Decoration ("dec" in margin or italics)   (5 pts each)

☐ alliteration _____ (5 pts)

MECHANICS

☐ banned words: go/went say/said _____ (-1 pt)

MORE ADVANCED ADDITIONS

☐ vocabulary words (*Label voc or bold.*) _____

☐ conversation _____

☐ simile _____

Total _____ /65

Custom total _____ / _____

Unit 3: Retelling Narrative Stories

Unit 3: Retelling Narrative Stories

Lesson 9: The Sword in the Stone

Literature Suggestion

With Lessons 9–13, read selected tales from *The Legend of King Arthur* by Roger Lancelyn Green (or a simpler version).

If you are returning work from Lesson 7 (Mohammed), read some of the elements of style students did well. Also, be sure everyone understands any corrections you may have noted.

Review

1. Read an alliteration you put in your story about Ali and the Sultan.

2. Play a vocabulary game from the TM to prepare for the quiz next week.

Pictionary on page 278 would be a good choice.

The next story you will write is probably one of the most famous medieval stories. It is part of the legend of King Arthur. Because it is lengthy, the brainstorming is broken into two parts.

It is recommended that young classes spend two weeks on this story. See below.

The Assignment

Day 1

1. Read "The Sword in the Stone," and outline Sections I and II on page 68.

2. Take turns telling back the story, one line of the outline at a time.

3. Brainstorm ideas for elements of style for Sections I and II on pages 69–70.

4. Note the vocabulary words for Lesson 9: *disclosed, contrite, scowl, dislodge*.

5. If time permits, outline and brainstorm ideas for Section III on pages 68 and 71. If not, continue next week, or complete this for homework according to your teacher's directions.

Days 2–4

1. Polish the Mohammed story from Lesson 7.

2. Write your own version of "The Sword in the Stone," using your key word outline and brainstorming ideas. Follow the checklist on page 72.

3. Cut out and learn the vocabulary words for Lesson 9. Review all.

Study for Vocabulary Quiz 2. It covers words from Lessons 1–9.

Source Text

The Sword in the Stone

I.

It was a cold Christmas morning in London. From all directions, people were streaming to the old church. Among them were Sir Ector, an elderly but respected knight, and his two sons, Sir Kay and Arthur. Sir Kay was a young, handsome knight, and 18-year-old Arthur was his squire. They filed into the church with everyone and took their seats.

II.

The people of London were troubled because their king had died, leaving no heir that anyone knew of. The question of who should be king was on everyone's mind and in everyone's prayers. The service began, and the archbishop spoke on and on. Then, suddenly, there was a great noise, and a burst of light blazed through the stained glass windows. Everyone rushed outside. To their surprise, a white marble stone sat in the churchyard. On it was a black anvil, and in the anvil was a glorious jeweled sword. The archbishop slowly approached the curious sight. He read the words inscribed in the stone:

WHOSO PULLETH THE SWORD OUT

OF THIS STONE IS RIGHTWISE

BORN KING OF ENGLAND

Of course, every knight tried to pull the sword from the stone. Though they strained with all their might, none succeeded. "Our king is not here," announced the archbishop. "We must tell every knight in the land about the sword in the stone."

III.

It was decided that on New Year's Day all the knights of England would come to London for a great tournament. After the tournament they would attempt to remove the sword from the stone. So, on New Year's Day Sir Ector, Sir Kay, and Arthur headed for London. They checked into the inn and headed for the tournament. As Kay's turn to fight neared, Arthur helped him on with his armor.

"Now hand me my sword," he said.

"The sword!" Arthur gasped. "It's not here. It must be back at the inn."

"Stupid boy! How can I fight without my sword?" Kay growled. "Go fetch it!"

Arthur knew there was no time for that, but he was not going to argue with Kay. He jumped on his horse and prayed for help. On the way to the inn, he passed the churchyard and saw the sword in the stone. There was the answer to his dilemma! *I'll just grab that sword*, he thought. He hopped off his horse and hastily pulled the sword from the stone. He rode to the tournament in time for the match and handed Kay the sword.

"That's not my sword!" Kay roared. Then he looked at it. "It's the sword from the stone!" he exclaimed. "How did you get this?"

Arthur explained what he had done. Everyone gathered around.

"The boy is lying," some said.

So the crowd took Arthur back to the old churchyard. They told Arthur to put the sword back into the stone, which he did easily.

Knight after knight tried to pull it back out, but it would not budge.

"Now, boy. You try," said Kay.

So Arthur reached for the sword and effortlessly pulled it from the stone. At that, all bowed down to him. "Hail to King Arthur," they said. And happiness was restored to the land that now had its rightful king.

Unit 3: Retelling Narrative Stories

The Story Sequence Chart

Setting, Characters, Background

What is the setting? Describe it. Who are the characters? Tell about them.	I. _London, Christmas_ 1. _cold, busy, ppl ➜ church_ 2. _Sir Ector, elderly, knight_ 3. _sons, Sir Kay, knight_ 4. _Arthur, squire, 18_

Plot or Problem

What is the problem? What do the characters do, say, think, and feel? What happens before the climax?	II. _ppl, ☹ b/c, king, XX, w/⊘ heir_ 1. _who, king?_ 2. _@ church, noise, light_ 3. _➜, ☉ ☉, (draw sword in stone), whoso, pulleth_ 4. _all, knights, tried, ⊘_

Climax and Resolution

What leads to the conflict being solved (the climax)? What happens as a result?	III. _New Year's, ➜ London_ 1. _tournament, then, pull_ 2. _Arthur, forgot, K, sword_ 3. _➜ get, ☉ ☉ church, grabbed_ 4. _"Not, mine! Where?"_ 5. _Arthur, explained, all ➜ ☉ ☉_ 6. _Arthur, ⬇⬆, all, bowed_

Institute for Excellence in Writing

Brainstorming Elements of Style

Sections I and II

Describing Settings

When you write a story, remember to use descriptions that appeal to the five senses. This is particularly important when describing the setting.

What would be seen, heard, or felt in London on Christmas morning? Describe these things in a way that tells what they look like, sound like, or feel like. For example, if you think of the road, you could write *Feet <u>shuffled</u> <u>rhythmically</u> on the <u>crowded</u>, <u>slushy</u> roads*. When you try to think of things to describe, consider the landscape, the weather, the buildings, the people. Include some strong verbs and -ly adverbs by asking what each *does*. Note the examples.

What would you see? *<u>Fresh</u> snow <u>encased</u> the <u>bare</u> trees; <u>empty</u> shops <u>lined</u> the streets.*

gray lines of smoke billowed; patches or clumps of snow dotted the streets, shimmering in the sunlight; masses of people

Hear?   *Bells <u>chimed</u> <u>continuously.</u>*

people chattered; carriages clattered and horses neighed; horses clip-clopped; children laughed as they played

Feel?   *<u>Frosty</u> air <u>stung</u> <u>sharply.</u>*

wet shoes plowed through snow; crowd pushed and shoved; warmth of the church welcomed

Section II

Describe the scenes in the church before and during the appearance of the stone, as well as the scene outside the church with the sword in the stone.

What would you see? *A <u>blast of brilliantly</u> <u>colored</u> light <u>instantly</u> <u>lit up</u> the <u>dark</u> church.*
What would it do?

rows of worshipers knelt reverently; burst of light; shattering of colored glass; massive white marble stone; radiant, jeweled sword

Hear?   *The monks <u>chanted</u> <u>melodiously.</u>*

din of a shower of shattered glass; thundering crash or boom; explosion; gasps, yells, cries

Feel?   *<u>Wooden</u> pews <u>trembled</u> <u>violently.</u>*

church quaked; blast or explosion of hot air; crowd pushing and shoving to see

Teams that match one of the samples given below get five tickets. (Or choose just one of each sample to be the winning simile.) Explain that these are not the "right" answers. They might not even be better than what the students come up with. They are just to add some fun to the brainstorming.

Unit 3: Retelling Narrative Stories

Alliteration

Write an idea for alliteration. If you are stuck, look at the things you wrote on page 69. Can you add words to any of them to form alliteration?

Here are a couple of ideas to get you started. Can you fill in the blanks with words that begin with the same sound? Try to include strong verbs and -ly adverbs.

The _____*whistling*_____ wind *whooshed and whirled wildly*_____ .

The _____*sparkling, sunlit*_____ snow *silently swirled*_____ .

Vocabulary Ideas

Having the vocabulary word chart on pages 260–261 in front of you will be helpful.

Have students turn to page 260. Offer a ticket for each vocabulary word they can use in a sentence that could be anywhere in the story. Encourage them to add vocabulary words to their stories. Here are a few ideas:

All of England was melancholy. The people were in anguish because they did not have a king.

All were intrigued and bewildered by the massive sword in the stone. It was incredible.

(Forms of words count; incredible is a form of credible.)

The crowning of a new king seemed imminent.

Section III Style

Describing Settings

Think about the scene at the tournament as well as at the churchyard.

What would you see? *White* tents *completely encircled* the *green* field.

crowds of excited people; fair ladies in long, flowing gowns; minstrels clad in colorful garb

Hear?   *Armor clanked.*

lively, melodious songs of bards; people laughing; horses galloping and neighing; announcer bellowing; knights heckling

Feel?   *wet, muddy ground*

cold, crisp air; crowds shoving; cold, hard metal armor; sharp swords

Smell or taste?   *disgustingly fetid horse stalls*

salty, crispy roast turkey legs; delicious, sweet breads and fruit-filled pies

Alliteration

Add a verb and an -ly adverb that both begin with an s to form alliteration. (Hint: Use the SRN -ly adverb list for help.)

The sword _____ _____ .

(Think about either when it was in the churchyard, when Arthur pulled it out, or when the others tried to do so.)

sat   silently, splendidly, solidly, solemnly, safely in the stone
stuck   stubbornly, steadfastly, securely in the stone.
slid   smoothly, successfully

Many ideas are given. Be sure students understand that they only need three words that begin with the same sound.

Lesson 9 Checklist - The Sword in the Stone

FORMAT

☐ Modified MLA format (See Appendix 1.)   _____ (5 pts)

STRUCTURE

☐ Title repeats or reflects key words from last sentence.   _____ (5 pts)

☐ Story Sequence Chart followed   _____ (5 pts)

STYLE Each section must contain at least one of each element of style.

¶ 1 ¶ 2 ¶ 3 **Dress-Ups (Underline one of each; abbreviate in right margin.)**   **(5 pts each)**

☐ ☐ ☐ -ly adverb   _____ (15 pts)

☐ ☐ ☐ *who–which* clause   _____ (15 pts)

☐ ☐ ☐ strong verb   _____ (15 pts)

      Decoration ("dec" in margin or italics)   **(5 pts each)**

☐ alliteration   _____ (5 pts)

MECHANICS

☐ banned words: go/went say/said   _____ (-1 pt)

MORE ADVANCED ADDITIONS

☐ vocabulary words (*Label voc or bold.*)   _____

☐ conversation   _____

☐ simile   _____

Total _____/65

Custom total _____ / _____

                                    Institute for Excellence in Writing

Tic-Tac-Toe: See Appendix 6, page 280. Use questions 1–9 on page 282. To last for two or three games, you may repeat some questions, add some of your own, or use vocabulary definitions.

Unit 3: Retelling Narrative Stories

Lesson 10: Borrowing a Conflict

Take Vocabulary Quiz 2.

Review

Play Tic-Tac-Toe from the TM.

Borrowing a Conflict

In this lesson, you will use what you have learned about stories to write an original story. You now know that every story must contain the basic elements of the Story Sequence Chart. Therefore, to help you write your story, you will first fill out the outline on page 76 with your own ideas, with the following qualifications: the setting must be during the Middle Ages, and the characters must be appropriate for that setting.

To further help, you may "borrow" a conflict from a familiar story. For example, what is the conflict of "The Three Little Pigs?" The pigs need to build houses to keep them safe from the big bad wolf. Two pigs are lazy and do not do a good job; one works hard and builds a strong house. His hard work is rewarded because the third pig's house is the only one that withstands the wolf's huffing and puffing. If you wanted to borrow this conflict for a Middle Ages story, you could change the characters to three knights and a fierce dragon. Instead of houses, the knights would build castles. (Or try three friendly dragons and an evil knight.)

Other stories that may work well are listed below with possible changes to make them appropriate to the Middle Ages. These are just sample ideas. You may think of your own.

"The Tortoise and the Hare"

The Foot Soldier and the Knight
Instead of a race, the soldier could beat the knight in a jousting tournament.

"The Boy Who Cried Wolf"

The Page Who Cried Dragon
The Dragon Who Cried Knight

"The Ant and the Grasshopper"

The Wise King and the Foolish King
Instead of preparing for winter, they could prepare (or not prepare) for attack.

"King Midas and the Golden Touch"

The King with the Magic Dub
Instead of everything he touches turning to gold, you could have every knight he dubs be possessed with a special power. To learn that this is not good, he could accidentally dub an evil knight.

To further help you understand this assignment, read the student sample in Appendix 3. Can you tell what familiar story it is based on?   *The Little Red Hen*

Unit 3: Retelling Narrative Stories

The Because Clause

As you write your story, use a new element of style: *the because clause*. The because clause is a clause (a group of words with a subject and a verb) that begins with the word *because*. Even though a because clause has a subject and a verb, it is not a complete sentence. Adding the word *because* to a sentence makes it an incomplete thought:

The knight saved the princess. (a sentence)

Because the knight saved the princess (not a sentence)

An entire because clause must be added to a sentence that is already complete. It may be added before or after the complete sentence. If the because clause comes first, follow it with a comma. Do not put a comma before a because clause.

To check that you have a complete sentence, remove the word *because*. You should have *two* sentences left. What are the two sentences in the samples in the box below?

> The kingdom rejoiced <u>because</u> the knight saved the princess.
>
> <u>Because</u> the knight saved the princess, the kingdom rejoiced.

A because clause helps add more detail to a sentence. It also helps explain why something happens. Try to add a because clause to each paragraph your write. When you do, underline the word *because*, and remember this comma rule:

> Place a comma *after* the entire because clause (unless there is a period there), but not usually *before* it.

Practice

Add more detail to each sentence by adding a because clause. You may add the clause to the beginning or the end of the sentence. Underline the word *because* since that is how you will indicate it in your paragraphs.

1. The knight mocked the foot soldier.

   The knight mocked the foot soldier <u>because</u> he had no horse or armor.

2. The foolish king did not prepare for the dragon's attack.

   The foolish king did not prepare for the dragon's attack <u>because</u> he was indolent and smug.

Institute for Excellence in Writing

These are vocabulary words from Lesson 20. It is okay for students to look ahead and use future words. Encourage it.

The Assignment

Day 1

1. Choose a familiar story from which you can "borrow a conflict." On page 76 begin to outline your idea for your own story. In a class setting, you may work in groups to get ideas flowing. What famous stories do all know?

2. Learn the new dress-up, the *because* clause, on page 74.

Days 2–4

1. Polish your "Ali and the Sultan's Saddle" story from Lesson 8.

2. Write your story. Be sure to include and label everything on the checklist on page 77. Attach the checklist to your final draft.

There are no new vocabulary words for this lesson. Continue to review and use words from Lessons 1–9.

Option for experienced students: Try the rhyming story described in the *Medieval History-Based Advanced Writing Lessons Blackline Masters*.

Each student's outline will be different.

The Story Sequence Chart

Setting, Characters, Background

What is the setting? Describe it. Who are the characters? Tell about them.

I. _____

   1. _____

   2. _____

   3. _____

   4. _____

Plot or Problem

What is the problem? What do the characters do, say, think, and feel? What happens before the climax?

II. _____

   1. _____

   2. _____

   3. _____

   4. _____

Climax and Resolution

What leads to the conflict being solved (the climax)? What happens as a result?

III. _____

   1. _____

   2. _____

   3. _____

   4. _____

Lesson 10 Checklist - Borrowing a Conflict

FORMAT

☐ Modified MLA format (See Appendix 1.)   _____ (5 pts)

STRUCTURE

☐ Title repeats or reflects key words from last sentence.   _____ (5 pts)

☐ Story Sequence Chart followed   _____ (5 pts)

STYLE Each section must contain at least one of each element of style.

¶ 1   ¶ 2   ¶ 3   **Dress-Ups (Underline one of each; abbreviate in right margin.)**   **(5 pts each)**

☐   ☐   ☐   -ly adverb   _____ (15 pts)

☐   ☐   ☐   *who–which* clause   _____ (15 pts)

☐   ☐   ☐   strong verb   _____ (15 pts)

☐   ☐   ☐   because clause   _____ (15 pts)

     Decoration ("dec" in margin or italics)   **(5 pts each)**

☐   alliteration   _____ (5 pts)

MECHANICS

☐ banned words: go/went say/said   _____ (-1 pt)

MORE ADVANCED ADDITIONS

☐ vocabulary words (*Label voc or bold.*)   _____

☐ conversation   _____

☐ simile   _____

Total _____ /80

Custom total _____ / _____

Unit 3: Retelling Narrative Stories

Teachers, review Unit 4: Summarizing a Reference in the TWSS workbook before teaching Lessons 11–15. If you have the seminar on DVD, watch the corresponding lesson.

Unit 4: Summarizing a Reference

Lesson 11: Alfred the Great

Review

1. Play hangman from the TM.

Use the phrase COMMA AFTER NOT BEFORE. (Once solved ask: Which clause needs a comma after it, but not before it? a because clause)

2. From the story you wrote for Lesson 10, read a sentence with a because clause. Did you add a comma? If so, where? If not, why not?

Reports: Topic Sentences and Clinchers

In the following lessons, you will be summarizing factual articles into short reports. When you are asked to write such a report, most often you would turn to an encyclopedia, textbook, or Internet article for information. In these lessons, the source texts will be provided.

How will you take notes for a summary report? Reports are not structured like stories, so you cannot use the Story Sequence Chart questions to help you outline from your source as we did in Unit 3 lessons. In addition, most sources will probably have much more information than you need, so it would not be practical to outline them by noting three words from every sentence as we did in Unit 2 lessons.

In this lesson you will learn a new way of outlining based on understanding that each paragraph in a report must have a clear topic. A topic is simply what the paragraph is about—the main idea of it. The paragraph should begin with a sentence that states the topic. All the details in the paragraph should support this topic sentence. Then, the paragraph should end with a sentence (a clincher) that restates the topic. Look at the sample paragraph below. What is the topic? (What is the paragraph about?)

> Most people of the Middle Ages were religious. By far the dominant religion in Europe was Catholicism. The Catholic Church had much power there during these times. But there were other religions practiced around the world, too. For example, there were Jews in many places. In the Middle East people were mostly believers of Islam. Taoism was one religion practiced in China, and Hinduism was in India. Many different religions were practiced during the Middle Ages.

Note that the first sentence (the topic sentence) and the last sentence (the clincher) tell the topic of the paragraph without saying anything like *The topic of the paragraph is* or *In this paragraph I will tell you about.*

Highlight the key words in the topic sentence and clincher that tell what the paragraph is about.

> #### Remember the topic-clincher rule:
> The topic sentence and clincher of a paragraph must repeat or reflect two to three key words.

The words must tell the topic of the paragraph. These words should be highlighted.

Unit 4: Summarizing a Reference

The Assignment

Day 1

1. Read the source text on page 82. With the help of your teacher, fill in an idea for a topic sentence. The topic is Alfred the Great, but what will you say about him? What is the main idea of the paragraph?

Example: Alfred G, ruler, A-Sax

2. Then, look for *no more than seven* interesting or important facts about Alfred the Great. Write each fact on one of the lines of the blank outline, using no more than three key words.

   Important: There is more information than you need for one summary paragraph. You will have to leave much out. Choose only the ideas that are the most important or most interesting. Think main ideas rather than specific details.

3. Tell back the meaning of each line of notes. Be sure you have a clear topic sentence and clincher. Remember to highlight them when you write your paragraph.

4. Go over the checklist on page 84. Be sure you understand everything on it.

5. Go over vocabulary words for Lesson 11: *prominent, myriad, virtue, endure.*

Days 2–4

1. Polish your "The Sword and the Stone" story from Lesson 9.

2. Before you write your paragraph, read over your notes to be sure you understand them. If something is unclear, look at the source text and fix the note.

3. Use your key word outline to write a paragraph about Alfred the Great. Remember that this is a summary, so you cannot include all of the facts in the source text. Follow the outline. *Do not look at the source text when you write.*

   Include and label everything on the checklist on page 84. Remember to highlight words in the topic sentence and clincher that tell the topic of the paragraph.

4. Cut out and learn vocabulary words for Lesson 11.

Unit 4: Summarizing a Reference

Source Text

Alfred the Great

Alfred the Great is the most famous ruler of the Anglo-Saxons. He was King of the West Saxons in Wessex, England, from 871–899. He actually had four older brothers who were king before him, but they all died. The crown, therefore, passed to him when he was only twenty-one years old. He is the only ruler of England to be called "the Great." He is best remembered for his clever, persistent fighting against Viking raiders. Vikings had conquered all of the Anglo-Saxon regions surrounding Wessex, but Alfred withstood their attacks. He is also remembered as the king who burned a peasant woman's cakes. A famous legend tells of a time when he was fleeing from the Vikings and came upon her cottage. The woman took him in as a stranger and asked him to watch her cakes while she tended to her animals. His mind was so busy planning an attack on the Vikings that the cakes burned, and she scolded him. How horrified she must have been when she discovered she had rebuked her king! Alfred was eventually able to defeat and make peace with the Vikings. In fact, he helped convert their king to Christianity. He ruled his kingdom well. He established schools and monasteries to educate his people. He worked hard to make his kingdom better. Some historians have called him "the most perfect character in history." Alfred was indeed a great ruler.

Circle *Alfred G, ruler, A-Sax* on the topic line to remind students to highlight these words or similar words in the topic sentences and clinchers of their paragraphs.

Key Word Outline - "Alfred the Great"

I. Topic: _____ *Alfred G, ruler, A-Sax* _____

1. _____ *crown, 21-y-o* _____

2. _____ *remembered, 4, fighting, vs. Vikings* _____

3. _____ *defeated, peace, w/Vikings* _____

4. _____ *converted, V, king, Christianity* _____

5. _____ *sch., monasteries, educate, people* _____

6. _____ *"perfect, character, history"* _____

Clincher

Lesson 11 Checklist - Alfred the Great

FORMAT

☐ Modified MLA format (See Appendix 1.) _____ (2 pts)

STRUCTURE

☐ Topic sentence with key words highlighted _____ (6 pts)

☐ Clincher with key words highlighted _____ (4 pts)

☐ Title repeats or reflects key words from last sentence. _____ (3 pts)

STYLE Each paragraph must contain at least one of each element of style.

Dress-Ups (Underline one of each; abbreviate in right margin.)   **(3 pts each)**

☐ -ly adverb _____ (3 pts)

☐ *who–which* clause _____ (3 pts)

☐ strong verb _____ (3 pts)

☐ because clause _____ (3 pts)

   Decoration ("dec" in margin or italics)   **(3 pts each)**

☐ alliteration _____ (3 pts)

MECHANICS

☐ banned words: go/went say/said _____ (-1 pt)

MORE ADVANCED ADDITIONS

☐ vocabulary words (*Label voc or bold.*) _____

☐ simile _____

Total _____/30

Custom total _____ / _____

Unit 4: Summarizing a Reference

Lesson 12: Charlemagne, Part 1

Review

In Lesson 11 you learned that reports are structured using paragraphs that have topic sentences and clinchers with key words that reveal their topics. Review pages 79–80 if necessary. You were asked to highlight these words in your paragraph(s).

1. Read the words you highlighted in your topic sentence and clincher of the paragraph about Alfred the Great.

2. Highlight the key words in the topic sentence and clincher that tell the topic of the following paragraph.

> Charles Martel, whose name means Charles the Hammer, ruled the Franks from 719 to 741. He received this nickname because of his persistent determination. He won the throne despite many enemies attempting to stop him—even throwing him in jail. When he was ruler, Islamic armies conquered Spain and planned to take his kingdom as well. But Charles defeated the invading armies and repeatedly attacked them. Thus, he was given the title by which he is remembered: Charles the Hammer.

In the next two lessons, you will repeat the steps you learned in Lesson 11 to write a 2-paragraph summary report about one of the greatest rulers of the Middle Ages: Charlemagne, grandson of Charles the Hammer.

Charlemagne

In this report, as in any report, every paragraph must have a clear topic. This means it must be about only one particular aspect of the subject. Your report will be organized into the following topics:

I.   Charlemagne, the Conqueror

II.   Charlemagne, the Founder of the Holy Roman Empire

Using the source text and blank outline on the following pages, follow the steps taught in Lesson 11 to write the first paragraph (Charlemagne the Conqueror). Be sure to limit your facts to those that support the topic. Which paragraph in the source text does not support the topic? Do not take notes from this paragraph. (For more detailed instructions, see the assignment on page 89.)

The last paragraph. It is about a tragic defeat.

Similes

A simile is a way to describe two unlike things using the words *like* or *as*. You have probably heard many familiar similes:

He is busy as a bee.   He eats like a bird (or pig).   She sings like a nightingale.

Learn more about similes in the decorations section of the SRN. You will practice this decoration on the brainstorming page.

Unit 4: Summarizing a Reference

Source Text

Charlemagne

Charlemagne, whose name means "Charles the Great," is one of the most famous rulers of the Middle Ages. He was born in A.D. 742, the son of King Pepin the Short, the grandson of Charles Martel. He and his brother inherited their kingdom and ruled the Franks, who lived in what is now France and part of Germany. However, when Charlemagne was twenty-six years old, his brother died, and Charlemagne became the sole ruler. As ruler, he became a mighty conqueror.

Charlemagne was deeply religious and was thought of as a kind and just man, but he was also a ruthless warrior. He wanted to expand his empire and spread his idea of the Christian faith everywhere. He is said to have ruled "by the sword and by the cross." For thirty years he fought many wars. By 800, his empire covered almost all of western Europe, from central Italy north to Denmark and from eastern Germany to the Atlantic Ocean. There had not been an empire so large since Ancient Rome. In fact, it was almost half the land of the old Roman Empire. Because of this, some people have called him the "Father of Europe."

Charlemagne also fought a war in Spain against the Muslims. In 778, the Muslims sent a message to Charlemagne saying that they desired peace. But when the king's army returned, the rear guard was ambushed between the mountains. Among those killed was their leader and one of Charlemagne's most trusted knights, Roland, his nephew. It was he who blew the horn to call Charlemagne back. When the king saw all his men dead, he was deeply angered and grieved. This incident became famous because an epic poem, *The Song of Roland*, was written about it. It was a tragic defeat.

Circle Charlemagne, conqueror in topic sentence to remind students to highlight these words or similar words in the topic sentences and clinchers of their paragraphs.

Key Word Outline - "Charlemagne"

I. Topic: <u>Charlemagne, conqueror</u>

(**Note:** *This is not how the source text begins. You must write a sentence about Charlemagne as a conqueror to begin your paragraph because that is your assigned topic.*)

1. *name, "Charles the Great"*

2. *kind, relig, + ruthless, warrior*

3. *wanted, expand, emp., Christianity*

4. *"ruled, sword, & cross"*

5. *30 yrs, wars ➔ by 800, most, W. Eur*

6. *largest, since, Rome*

Clincher

Rough Draft Checklist

☐ Topic sentence *(Highlight key words that tell the topic.)*

<u>Dress-Ups (Underline.)</u>

☐ -ly adverb   ☐ *who-which*   ☐ strong verb   ☐ because clause

☐ No banned verbs: go/went say/said   ☐ vocabulary words

Choose one decoration (label in right margin):   ☐ alliteration   ☐ simile

☐ Clincher *(Highlight two to three key words from topic sentence.)*

Brainstorming Elements of Style

Because Clause

Add more detail to each sentence by adding a because clause. You may add the clause to the beginning or the end of the sentence. Underline the word *because* since that is how you will indicate it in your paragraphs.

1. Charlemagne fought many wars.

   Because he wanted a giant empire, Charlemagne fought many wars.

2. Charlemagne was called "the Father of Europe."

   Charlemagne was called "the Father of Europe" because he conquered most of its land.

Similes

Recall that a simile is a way to compare two unlike things using the words *like* or *as*. Write a simile or two about Charlemagne. What about the conqueror Charlemagne was great?

Charlemagne's empire seemed as endless as   *the sun's rays, the sea, the sky*   .

Lesson 12: Charlemagne, Part 1

The Assignment

Day 1

1. Read the source text (page 86). Use page 87 to make a key word outline. Notice that on the topic line there are key words that remind you to write a sentence about Charlemagne being a conqueror. The source text may not begin this way, but you must begin with a clear sentence that tells the topic.

    Highlight or circle these words to remind you to highlight them when you write your paragraph.

    Next, with the help of your teacher, look for *no more than seven* interesting or important facts *about the topic*. Do not take notes from every sentence. Look only for facts that support the topic. You will have to leave some information out. What information does not tell about him being a conqueror?

The last paragraph that tells about his greatest defeat could certainly be omitted from a paragraph about him being a great conqueror.

2. Look at the vocabulary words for Lesson 12: *uniform, perturbed, foremost, reform.*

Days 2–4

1. Polish your story from Lesson 10.

2. Use your key word outline on page 87 to write a rough draft paragraph. Start with a sentence that includes the words *Charlemagne* and *conqueror* (or synonyms). This will let your reader know the topic of the paragraph. Do not say anything like "In this paragraph" or "This report is about."

3. Include and label everything on the rough checklist below the outline.

4. End your paragraph with a sentence that reminds your reader of the topic. To do this, repeat or reflect two to three key words from the topic sentence in your last sentence. We call this sentence the *clincher*.

5. **Highlight** the words in the topic sentence and clincher that repeat or reflect the same ideas and tell the topic.

6. In Lesson 13 we will add the second paragraph.

7. Cut out and learn vocabulary words for Lesson 12.

Option for experienced students: You may follow the same procedure for a second paragraph (Charlemagne the Reformer) using pages from the *Medieval History-Based Advanced Writing Lessons Blackline Masters*.

Charlemagne

In a class setting, students can trade rough drafts from Lesson 12. With the teacher's direction, they should check their classmate's report for all required elements, labeled as instructed. Especially check that the paragraph has a clear topic sentence and clincher with key words highlighted. This is not a grading time, but a time for students to help one another. Teachers should ask for some students to share topic sentences and clinchers. *Do not collect the paragraphs from Lesson 12 as they will be needed in this lesson.*

Unit 4: Summarizing a Reference

Lesson 13: Charlemagne, Part 2

Review

1. Play a vocabulary game from the TM to prepare for the quiz in Lesson 14.

2. Share your topic sentence and clincher from the paragraph you wrote in Lesson 12. What words did you highlight?

The Assignment

Day 1

1. Follow the procedure taught in Lessons 11–12 to outline a second paragraph about Charlemagne (the founder of the Holy Roman Empire). Use the source text and blank outline on the following pages.

2. After you have outlined the paragraph, read page 94 to learn how to put all your Charlemagne paragraphs together into one report.

   Add an idea for an introductory sentence to the beginning of the first paragraph (Charlemagne as conqueror). Add an idea for a final clincher to the end of the final paragraph (founder of the Holy Roman Empire).

3. Look at vocabulary words for Lesson 13: *bestow, devout, renowned, proficient.*

Days 2–4

1. Polish your Alfred the Great report from Lesson 11.

2. Using the outline on page 93, write the final paragraph of your Charlemagne report.

3. Put both of your paragraphs about Charlemagne together into one report. See page 94 for help adding an introductory sentence and final clincher to this report.

4. Follow and attach the final checklist to your report (see page 95).

5. Cut out and learn the new vocabulary words. Review all.

> Study for Vocabulary Quiz 3. It covers Lessons 1–13.

Unit 4: Summarizing a Reference

Source Text

Charlemagne: Founder of the Holy Roman Empire

During his reign, Charlemagne significantly extended the power and influence of the Roman Catholic Church. He gave much land and money to it. He had many new churches built all over his kingdom. He was known as the protector of the church. In addition, he protected Pope Leo III from rebels who had tried to attack him.

On Christmas Day in the year 800, Charlemagne traveled to St. Peter's Basilica in Rome to worship. As he knelt at the altar to pray, Pope Leo III approached with a beautiful golden crown. He placed the crown on the king's head and declared him "Emperor of the Romans." It was a public declaration of the support the pope and Charlemagne had for each other.

Legend says that Charlemagne knew nothing of Pope Leo's plan to declare him emperor. Regardless, he accepted the crown. While his new title did not give him any more power than he already had, it did make him more determined to expand the church throughout the empire. Today Charlemagne is remembered as the founder of the Holy Roman Empire.

Key Word Outline - "Charlemagne: Founder of the Holy Roman Empire"

I. Topic: Charlemagne, founder, Holy Roman Empire

1. ↑, power, influence, Rom Cath Church

2. gave, land, $

3. known, protector, Church

4. Christmas 800 → St. Peter's Basilica, Rome

5. Pope Leo III, crowned, "Emp. of Romans"

6. = support, Pope, Charl, ea other

7. → Charl, determined, expand, Church

Clincher
Final clincher (see next page)

Rough Draft Checklist

☐ Topic sentence *(Highlight key words that tell the topic.)*

  Dress-Ups (Underline.)

  ☐ -ly adverb   ☐ *who–which*   ☐ strong verb   ☐ because clause

  ☐ No banned verbs: go/went say/said

  Choose one decoration (label in right margin):   ☐ alliteration   ☐ simile

  ☐ vocabulary words

☐ Clincher *(Highlight two to three key words from topic sentence.)*

Putting It All Together

Once you have written the paragraph about Charlemagne as the founder of the Holy Roman Empire, you will have two paragraphs about Charlemagne. You must combine both the paragraphs into one report.

The Introductory Statement

At the beginning of your first paragraph, *before* the topic sentence about Charlemagne as a conqueror, you must add a sentence that introduces the subject of the entire report. If you do not, it will appear that the entire report will be about him as a conqueror.

Here is a sample. Words that show the subject of the entire report are in bold. The highlighted words show the topic of the paragraph. (Your topic sentence may need to change slightly to make the introductory sentence and topic sentence flow together well. In the example below, *Charlemagne* was changed to *he* to avoid repetition of his name.)

> **Charlemagne** is one of the most **renowned rulers** of the early Middle Ages. *He*
>
> was a mighty *conqueror*.

Teachers, be sure to go over the checklist with students, especially the structure requirements.

Discuss ideas with the class. Help as necessary. Walk around the room to see and comment on the ideas students are writing. Help them smoothly connect their introductory sentence to the first topic sentence. Here are some ideas for introductory sentences:

Charlemagne, King of the Franks, once ruled a massive empire in Europe.

Charlemagne was one of the greatest kings of the Middle Ages.

Charlemagne controlled much of Europe in the late 700s.

Charlemagne, founder of the Holy Roman Empire, fought hard to expand his empire.

The Final Clincher

You must also end your entire report by repeating the subject. We call this the *final clincher*. You create your final clincher by repeating or reflecting key words from your *introductory statement* after the clincher of the last paragraph.

> Charlemagne's most remembered title is *"Founder of the Holy Roman Empire."* **He**
>
> was a **magnificent ruler**.

The introductory statement and final clincher are like a topic sentence and clincher of a paragraph, but for the entire report. Notice how they are used in the student sample in Appendix 3, page 233.

If using decorations in reports is difficult for your students, have them cross this requirement off. Students will return to practicing decorations in Unit 5: Writing from Pictures.

Lesson 13 Checklist - Charlemagne, Part 2

FORMAT

☐ Modified MLA format (See Appendix 1.) _____ (3 pts)

STRUCTURE

☐ Introductory statement (no highlights) _____ (5 pts)

☐ ☐ Topic sentences with key words highlighted, each paragraph _____ (5 pts)

☐ ☐ Clinchers with key words highlighted, each paragraph _____ (5 pts)

☐ Final clincher reflects introductory statement (no highlights). _____ (2 pts)

☐ Title repeats or reflects key words from final clincher. _____ (2 pts)

STYLE Each paragraph must contain at least one of each element of style.

¶ 1 ¶ 2 **Dress-Ups (Underline one of each; abbreviate in right margin.)**   **(3 pts each)**

☐ ☐ -ly adverb _____ (6 pts)

☐ ☐ *who-which* clause _____ (6 pts)

☐ ☐ strong verb _____ (6 pts)

☐ ☐ because clause _____ (6 pts)

Decorations (at least one per para.) ("dec" in margin or italics)   **(2 pts each)**

☐ alliteration, simile _____ (4 pts)

MECHANICS

☐ banned words: go/went say/said _____ (-1 pt)

MORE ADVANCED ADDITIONS

☐ vocabulary words (*Label voc or bold.*) _____

☐ advanced paragraph- Charlemagne the Reformer _____

Total _____ /50

Custom total _____ / _____

Unit 4: Summarizing a Reference

Unit 4: Summarizing a Reference

Lesson 14: Vikings

Take Vocabulary Quiz 3.

Review

Read the introductory sentence and final clincher of your Charlemagne report.

Remember that we use these to tie together 2- or 3-paragraph reports. In such reports, each paragraph has its own topic, but the topics relate to one subject. The introductory sentence and final clincher tell the subject of the entire report.

In this lesson you will follow the instructions in Lessons 11–13 to write a report about Vikings. You will write one paragraph.

The Assignment

Day 1

1. Read the source text on the following page. Even though it is two paragraphs, choose the facts you want from it in order to write one paragraph about Vikings as fierce warriors or raiders. You are summarizing. Write the facts in key word notes on the blank outline.

2. In your own words, tell the meaning of each line of your notes.

Days 2–4.

1. Use your key word outline to write your report.

2. Remember to highlight words in your topic sentence and clincher that tell the topic of the paragraph.

3. There are no new vocabulary words for this lesson.

Option for experienced students: Those who are ready to write a 2- or 3-paragraph report should follow the instructions in the *Medieval History-Based Advanced Writing Lessons Blackline Masters.*

Literature Suggestion

With Lessons 14–17 read *The King's Shadow* by Elizabeth Alder.

Source Text

Vikings

The Norsemen, also known as Vikings, lived in Scandinavia but traveled much during the Middle Ages. They are mostly remembered as fierce warriors who savagely attacked much of Europe from the 700s until about 1100. Their land could not support them, so they attacked, looted, and invaded other European countries. What they did not steal, they burned. They killed women and children as well as men. The most savage of these Viking warriors were called *berserker*. They were like raging madmen. The term *berserk*, which now is used to describe someone who is acting wildly, originated from this name for Viking warriors. The Vikings were so feared that churches in Europe had a special prayer for protection: "God deliver us from the fury of the Norsemen."

Most Viking attacks were made by small groups of warriors who raided defenseless small towns, farms, and churches. They were seeking cattle, horses, food, and valuables such as the gold, silver, and ivory decorations in churches. Sometimes, however, the warriors wanted to take land. To do this, they sent several hundred warships. In these attacks, the Vikings were able to gain parts of England and France. Everywhere they went, Viking warriors struck fear in people.

Key Word Outline - "Vikings"

I. Topic: Vikings, fierce, warriors

1. *lived, Scandinavia*

2. *attacked, Eur, 700s-1100*

3. *looted, killed, burned*

4. *most, savage, beserker*

5. *most, sm groups, surprise*

6. *animals, food, valuables*

7. *want, land, 100s warships*

Clincher

Unit 4: Summarizing a Reference

Lesson 14 Checklist - Vikings

FORMAT

- [ ] Modified MLA format (See Appendix 1.)   _____ (2 pts)

STRUCTURE

- [ ] Topic sentence with key words highlighted   _____ (6 pts)
- [ ] Clincher with key words highlighted   _____ (6 pts)
- [ ] Title repeats or reflects key words from final clincher.   _____ (2 pts)

STYLE Each paragraph must contain at least one of each element of style.

Dress-Ups (Underline one of each; abbreviate in right margin.)   **(3 pts each)**

- [ ] -ly adverb   _____ (3 pts)
- [ ] _who–which_ clause   _____ (3 pts)
- [ ] strong verb   _____ (3 pts)
- [ ] because clause   _____ (3 pts)

Decorations (Choose one.) ("dec" in margin or italics)   **(2 pts each)**

- [ ] alliteration or simile   _____ (2 pts)

MECHANICS

- [ ] banned words: go/went say/said   _____ (-1 pt)

MORE ADVANCED ADDITIONS

- [ ] vocabulary words (_Label voc or bold._)   _____
- [ ] advanced paragraph(s)- Viking Explorers; a third topic   _____
- [ ] introductory sentence   _____
- [ ] final clincher   _____

Total _____/30

Custom total _____ / _____

Unit 4: Summarizing a Reference

Lesson 15: A Year to Remember: The Battle of Hastings

Review

Play a review game like Tic-Tac-Toe or 21 Questions from the TM.

Use questions 1–17 on page 282 plus some vocabulary words if needed.

The Assignment

Day 1

1. Read the source text on the following page. Choose the facts you want from it in order to write a paragraph about the Battle of Hastings. Write them in key word notes on the blank outline. Be sure to include the Battle of Hastings in your topic sentence because that is the topic of this paragraph.

2. In your own words, tell the meaning of each line of your notes.

Days 2–4

1. Polish your Charlemagne report from Lesson 13.

2. Use your key word outline to write a summary report.

3. Remember to highlight words in your topic sentence and clincher that tell the topic of the paragraph.

4. Cut out and learn the vocabulary words for Lesson 15.

Option for experienced students: Students who are ready to write a 2-paragraph report should follow the instructions in the *Medieval History-Based Advanced Lessons Blackline Masters*.

Unit 4: Summarizing a Reference

Source Text

A Year to Remember: The Battle of Hastings

The year 1066 is a famous year in history because in it the Battle of Hastings was fought. It was a battle over the throne of England. It was fought because William, the Duke of Normandy in France, claimed that King Edward had made him his heir. (They were cousins.) However, after the king died, the people of England crowned Harold Godwinson, who was the king's brother-in-law. William immediately headed for England with his army. Harold prepared for battle. He had his men build barricades of tree trunks. Then the soldiers armed themselves with double-edged axes and spears and lined up on the hillside. On October 14, William's forces met Harold's forces on a hill near the town of Hastings. A long and difficult battle followed. It lasted all day until an arrow struck and killed Harold. Some legends say the arrow struck him in the eye. The Normans won the battle, and William headed to London. He was crowned King of England on the following Christmas Day. That great battle of 1066 gave England a new king—a Norman king.

A Norman Soldier

Institute for Excellence in Writing

Key Word Outline - "A Year to Remember: The Battle of Hastings"

I. Topic: Battle of Hastings, famous, Eng, 1066

1. over, throne, Eng

2. Will, Dk Normandy, claimed, 👑 heir

3. 👑, XX, Harold, crowned

4. Wm ➜ Eng., battle

5. Oct. 14, fought, Harold, XX

6. Wm ➜ London

7. crowned, Christmas, 1066

Clincher

Lesson 15 Checklist -
A Year to Remember: The Battle of Hastings

FORMAT

☐ Modified MLA format (See Appendix 1.) _____ (3 pts)

STRUCTURE

☐ Topic sentence with key words highlighted _____ (5 pts)

☐ Clincher with key words highlighted _____ (5 pts)

☐ Title repeats or reflects key words from final clincher. _____ (2 pts)

STYLE Each paragraph must contain at least one of each element of style.

Dress-Ups (Underline one of each; abbreviate in right margin.)   **(2 pts each)**

☐ -ly adverb _____ (2 pts)

☐ *who-which* clause _____ (2 pts)

☐ strong verb _____ (2 pts)

☐ because clause _____ (2 pts)

Decorations (Choose one.) ("dec" in margin or italics)   **(2 pts each)**

☐ alliteration or simile _____ (2 pts)

MECHANICS

☐ banned words: go/went say/said _____ (-1 pt)

MORE ADVANCED ADDITIONS

☐ vocabulary words (*Label voc or bold.*) _____

☐ advanced paragraph- William the Conqueror _____

☐ introductory sentence _____

☐ final clincher _____

Total _____25

Custom total _____ / _____

Teachers, review Unit 5: Writing from Pictures in the TWSS workbook before teaching Lessons 16–17. If you have the seminar on DVD, watch the corresponding lesson.

Lesson 16: The Magic Lamp

Unit 5: Writing from Pictures

Lesson 16: The Magic Lamp

Review

Stretch the following sentence by adding each element of style as your teacher instructs.

Instruct students to write the following sentence sideways on a piece of paper (landscape orientation) with spaces between the words.

Ali   went   into   the   cave

Ali went into the cave.

Put each of the following on the whiteboard, one at a time. Each time, instruct the students to add the element to their sentence using a ^. Explain that while they will not usually add all dress-ups to a single sentence, this exercise gives them practice at using and punctuating each. It is also fun!

☐ w-w clause (Remind them to place a comma before and after.)

☐ b/c clause (Review comma rule: after the clause, usually not before it.)

☐ strong verb (Replace *went*.)

☐ -ly adverb

☐ vocab word or decoration (alliteration or simile)

Sample: Ali, <u>who</u> feared for his life, <u>scrambled</u> <u>frantically</u> into the cold, <u>creepy</u> cave <u>because</u> there was no place else to hide.

In this lesson you will learn to write from pictures rather than from source texts. But before you do, learn a new dress-up: the quality adjective.

Quality Adjectives

Today, learn another IEW dress-up that is a describing word: the *quality adjective.*

An adjective is a word that describes a noun—a person, place, or thing. Adjectives tell things like *what color, what size, what shape, what kind, how many.* Most adjectives can be put into a phrase like this:

the _____ thing (or person)

Can you think of some adjectives to describe the things you see around you? Can you add an adjective to the sentence you stretched? (Hint: Describe Ali or the cave.)

Many of your vocabulary words are adjectives. Can you use some to describe a person, place, or thing?

Have students turn to pages 260–261 and try to use some vocabulary words to describe people or things.

Banned Adjectives

Descriptive words like adjectives make your writing more enjoyable; however, there are some adjectives that are overused or boring. You do not want to use these. Look at the sentences below. Underline the adjectives. Which are boring adjectives and which are quality adjectives? Which are more precise?

He was a <u>mean</u> sultan. He was a <u>surly</u> sultan.

The lamp held a <u>nice</u> genie. The lamp held a <u>benevolent</u> genie.

Two banned adjectives are listed in the box below. Memorize them.

Banned Adjectives

nice, mean

When you write, be sure *not* to use these words or words like them. When you are tempted to use one of them, go to a thesaurus or the quality adjective section in the *Student Resource Notebook* to help you replace it with a stronger adjective. You should tab that section of the SRN.

Replace the banned adjectives with quality adjectives in these sentences.

Encourage students to choose the words that best communicate the image or meaning desired. Discourage them from just shouting out any words on the lists.

1. The nice lamp sparkled throughout the big cave.

   Example: The glorious lamp sparkled throughout the vast cave.

2. The king's guard seemed like mean men.

   Example: The king's guard seemed like cruel men.

Past Perfect Tense

The story you will be writing for this lesson should be written in past tense. However, you may also find the past perfect tense, which is the past of past tense, very helpful.

The past perfect tense is formed by placing the word *had* in front of a past tense verb. The past perfect tense is used when you want to write about what happened before what you are writing about in past tense.

When writing from pictures, you must begin each paragraph with what you see in each picture. For the first picture of this lesson, you might write something like this:

   Abu was running for his life as arrows whizzed by his head.

Then, if you want to tell what happened before this, such as why he is running, you must switch to past perfect by putting the word had in front of the past tense verbs:

   *Abu was running for his life as arrows whizzed by his head. Clearly he **had angered***

   *the king's guard, but he **had not meant** to so do. Now as he was running, he was praying*

   for help and looking for any place to hide.

Notice that the last sentence switched back to regular past tense. Why?

   It returned to telling what is in the picture, not what was before it.

Writing from Pictures

In this lesson you will write a story based on three pictures. To do so, follow the assignment instructions. Be sure to add quality adjectives to your story!

The Assignment

Day 1

1. Look at the three pictures on page 109. On the top blank next to the first picture, write what is happening in the picture (the central fact) in key words.

   On the other lines by the first box, you will have to explain in more detail what is happening by answering questions such as those on page 108. Write in key word notes.

2. Repeat the above steps for the remaining two pictures.

3. Brainstorm some elements of style on page 110. Be sure to do the vocabulary. It will help prepare you for the quiz next class.

4. Begin composing a class version of the story orally as the teacher writes it on a whiteboard. Write just enough to be sure everyone understands the process.

Teachers should ask more specific questions based on answers to some of the general questions. Write class ideas on a whiteboard, but do not have students copy them. The class exercise is to demonstrate the process. Students will ask and answer their own questions at home to create their own stories. Also, as you discuss ideas, talk about possible dress-ups or decorations.

Days 2–4

1. Polish the Vikings report from Lesson 14.

2. Outline a story from pictures in the same way we did in class; then, write your story in three paragraphs. Each should begin with the central fact of one of the pictures (highlighted).

3. Try to add all the elements of style listed on the checklist. Remember to highlight words in the topic sentence that tell what is happening in each picture. Highlight clinchers as well.

4. Cut out and learn vocabulary words for Lesson 16.

Advanced stylistic technique for experienced students who find adjectives easy: *See the Medieval History-Based Advanced Lessons Blackline Masters* to learn about dual dress-ups.

Study for Vocabulary Quiz 4. It will cover words from Lessons 1–16.

Questions for Writing from Pictures

These questions are sample ideas. You do not have to answer all of them, nor do they have to be answered in order. You may also think of others as well.

I.   What is happening in the picture?

 What is he doing? What is he thinking?

 How does he feel?

 Where is he? Describe the setting.

 What happened before the picture to cause this scene?

 Are there people we cannot see? What are they doing? Feeling? Thinking?

II.   What is happening in the picture?

 What is the character doing?

 What is he thinking and feeling?

 What will he do next? Why?

 What will he see? Feel? Describe.

III. What is happening in the picture?

 What is the character doing?

 What is he thinking and feeling?

 Are there other people or things there that are not pictured?

 What are they like? Doing?

 What will the character do next? Why?

 How will it all end?

Key Word Outline

I.   Central fact: _Abul, flee, invaders_
   village, stunned, attack
   arrows, whiz, ♡, pound
   wondered, who, why
   where, go?

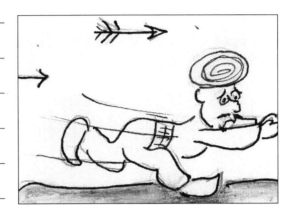

Clincher

II. Central fact: _reached, mysterious, cave_
   rumors, haunted, should, ➔?
   arrow, whiz, jump, ➔
   dark, still, quiet
   wandered, maze, ➔ lg chamb
   ⊙ ⊙, gold, jewels

Clincher

III. Central fact: _p/u, lamp, dust, ⬆_
   shook, exploded
   genie, "3 wishes"
   1, save, village
   2, keep, safe, prosperous
   3, free, self, b friend

Clincher

Brainstorming Elements of Style

Quality Adjectives

Describe the following things using quality adjectives. Think about describing what things would look like, sound like, or feel (sense of touch) like. When describing people, think about how they would feel (emotions).

arrows: _sharp, fast, deadly, numerous, horrifying, frightening_

the man (in each scene): _terrified, panicked, relieved, curious, stunned, doubtful, dubious_

cave: _dark, cool, hidden, serene, quiet, remote_

lamp: _dusty, golden, dented, metallic, radiant, sleek, stunning_

Strong Verbs and -ly Adverbs

Use strong verbs with -ly adverbs to tell what each of the following would be doing.

arrows: _whooshed and whizzed; flew; pierced—relentlessly; interminably_

the man (in each scene): _fled, panting, gazed, beheld, studied curiously, explored, dared, rubbed, hoped; quickly, rashly_

lamp: _sat, tantalized, sparkled, glowed; silently elegantly, radiantly, gloriously_

Alliteration

(Hint: Choose some of the dress-ups above, and add to them. For example, if your adjective for arrows was dreadful, *you could add* deadly *for* dreadful, deadly *arrows. If your verb was* whizzed, *you could add* wildly *for* whizzed wildly.)

a few, fast, frightening arrows; glorious, golden lamp glowed; rashly rubbed the radiant lamp

Similes

Can you finish one of these simile ideas?

Arrows whizzed (or buzzed) around him like _nuclear mosquitoes, bullets, miniature missiles_

The lamp _____ like _____
sat like a king on a throne; glowed like the sun; spewed smoke like a volcano

Vocabulary Words

Which vocabulary words might you be able to use in the story. How? See pages 260–261.

    Institute for Excellence in Writing

Give a ticket for each word a student can use in a sentence that could be in this story. This will be a good review for the quiz next class. Here are some ideas:

Arrows flew <u>interminably</u>.

He would not be <u>apprehended</u>.

"This is <u>ludicrous</u>," the <u>perturbed</u> man thought. "I did nothing to cause me to have to <u>endure</u> such treatment."

Thankfully, the archers were not <u>proficient</u>.

The genie warned him not to request <u>capriciously</u> so that he might <u>bestow</u> a precious gift on him.

Lesson 16 Checklist - The Magic Lamp

FORMAT

☐ Modified MLA format (See Appendix 1.) _____ (2 pts)

STRUCTURE

☐ ☐ ☐ Topic sentences with key words highlighted, each paragraph _____ (6 pts)

☐ ☐ ☐ Clinchers with key words highlighted, each paragraph _____ (5 pts)

☐ Title repeats or reflects key words from final clincher. _____ (3 pts)

STYLE Each paragraph must contain at least one of each element of style.

¶ 1 ¶ 2 ¶ 3 Dress-Ups (Underline one of each; abbreviate in right margin.)	(2 pts each)
☐ ☐ ☐ -ly adverb	_____ (6 pts)
☐ ☐ ☐ *who–which* clause	_____ (6 pts)
☐ ☐ ☐ strong verb	_____ (6 pts)
☐ ☐ ☐ because clause	_____ (6 pts)
☐ ☐ ☐ quality adjective	_____ (6 pts)
Decorations (Use at least one per para.) ("dec" in margin or italics)	(2 pts each)
☐ alliteration	_____ (2 pts)
☐ simile	_____ (2 pts)
☐ _____	_____ (2 pts)

MECHANICS

☐ banned words: go/went say/said nice/mean _____ (-1 pt)

MORE ADVANCED ADDITIONS

☐ vocabulary words (*Label voc or bold.*) _____

☐ conversation _____

☐ dual adjective, verb, or -ly adverb _____

Total _____ /52

Custom total _____ / _____

Unit 5: Writing from Pictures

UNIT 5: Writing from Pictures

Lesson 17: The King and the Dragon

Take Vocabulary Quiz 4.

Review

Allow time for some students to read their stories.

The 3sss

In this lesson you will write another story from pictures just as you did in Lesson 16. Before you do, though, learn a new decoration that will be fun to add to it: a 3sss.

The name 3sss stands for short, staccato sentences. The 3sss is simply the use of three short sentences (no more than five words each) in a row. Using short sentences in the middle of longer sentences can be a powerful way to draw attention to the short sentences, so use short sentences for important parts of a story. Here is a sample:

> The dragon terrorized the town every day. *It swooped over the city. It spit*   dec.
>
> *fire. It left devastation.*

Caution: The sentences must be complete sentences with a subject and a verb. Do not create fragments.

You will brainstorm ideas for a 3sss as well as the other two decorations after you outline your story; however, only two of the three will be required in your story. Having the extra one to choose from will allow you to use the two you like best.

Play the Sentence Stretching Game in Appendix 6. Add extra 3sss cards to be sure at least some choose it.

Unit 5: Writing from Pictures

The Assignment

Day 1

1. Look at the three pictures on page 115. On the top blank next to the first picture, write what is happening in the picture (the central fact) in key words.

2. On the other lines by the first box, you will have to explain in more detail what is happening by answering questions such as those below. Write in key word notes.

Teachers should ask more specific questions based on answers to some of the general questions. Write class ideas on a whiteboard, but do not have students copy them. They may fill in their own ideas instead. Students will ask and answer more of their own questions at home to create their own stories. Also, as you discuss ideas, talk about possible dress-ups or decorations.

3. Repeat the above steps for the remaining two pictures.

4. Brainstorm some elements of style on page 116.

Days 2–4

1. Polish the "Year to Remember" report from Lesson 15.

2. Finish your outline of a story from pictures; then, write your story in three paragraphs. Each should begin with the central fact of one of the pictures (highlighted).

3. Try to add all the elements of style listed on the checklist. Remember to highlight words in the topic sentence that tell what is happening in each picture. Highlight clinchers as well.

4. Cut out and learn vocabulary words for Lesson 17.

Advanced stylistic technique for experienced students: See the *Medieval History-Based Advanced Lessons Blackline Masters* to learn the triple extension.

Possible Questions for Writing from Pictures

What is happening in the picture?

Describe the character(s).

What are they doing? What are they thinking? Why?

How are they feeling? Why? How are their feelings being shown?

What happened just before the event?

Where is the event happening?

What would you see, hear, or feel?

What is happening around the scene (not in the picture)?

Are there other characters who are not pictured?

What will happen after the event in the picture?

Key Word Outline

I.   Central fact: *king, ☹, brooding*

dragon, swooping, w/fire

worried, attack

knights, away

summoned, squire, knighted

Clincher

II. Central fact: *new, kn-, hid, rock*

⊙ ⊙, dragon, ☹

"Why, terrorizing?"

"What? Want, play"

ppl, run, ⊘ friends

Clincher

III. Central fact: *kn-, befriend, back*

rtn, castle, "⊘, fear"

king, amazed

"dragon, wants, friends"

"guard, castle?"

king's, pet

Clincher

Brainstorming Elements of Style

Quality Adjectives

Describe the following things using quality adjectives. Think about describing what things would look like, sound like, or feel (sense of touch) like. When describing people, think about how they would feel (emotions).

king: *anxious, worried, distraught, irate, perturbed, melancholy, helpless, hopeful, surprised, relieved*

the dragon (each picture): *fierce, massive, playful, friendly, frisky, spirited, timid, kind, loyal, peaceful, distressed, dreaded, tame*

knight: *young, naïve, frightened, nervous, petrified, curious, relieved, trusting, gentle, noble*

Strong Verbs and -ly Adverbs

Use strong verbs with -ly adverbs.

king: *scowled angrily; sulked; brooded; summoned resolutely; waited nervously; announced happily*

the dragon (each picture): *taunted and teased interminably; playfully swooped; soared innocently; bore the knight*

knight: *searched; ascended; hid and cowered nervously; trembled; knelt; neared nervously; coaxed gently and wisely*

Decorations

Can you think of decorations you might be able to add to your story?

3sss Ideas

Note: If the 3sss is difficult for a student, he or she may opt to omit it.

Alliteration Ideas

noble knight knelt nervously; serpent swooped and soared; dragon tame and timid

Simile Ideas

The knight cowered behind a rock like *a frightened kitten; a frightened child; a sissy*

Other Ideas

Vocabulary Words

Which vocabulary words might you be able to use in the story. How? See pages 260–261.

Give a ticket for each word a student can use in a sentence that could be in this story. Here are some ideas:

The <u>ludicrous</u> dragon flew <u>capriciously</u> over the otherwise <u>serene</u> kingdom, <u>plummeting</u> toward the castle and <u>spewing</u> fire.

The <u>perturbed</u> king believed <u>tragedy</u> was <u>imminent</u>.

He needed a <u>proficient</u> knight, but all the <u>renowned</u> warriors were away.

The dragon <u>reformed</u> his ways.

The king <u>extolled</u> the young, <u>intrepid</u> knight.

Lesson 17 Checklist - The King and the Dragon

FORMAT

☐ Modified MLA format (See Appendix 1.)   _____ (2 pts)

STRUCTURE

☐ ☐ ☐ Topic sentences with key words highlighted, each paragraph   _____ (6 pts)

☐ ☐ ☐ Clinchers with key words highlighted, each paragraph   _____ (3 pts)

☐ Title repeats or reflects key words from final clincher.   _____ (3 pts)

STYLE Each paragraph must contain at least one of each element of style.

¶ 1   ¶ 2   ¶ 3   **Dress-Ups (Underline one of each; abbreviate in right margin.)**   **(2 pts each)**

☐ ☐ ☐ -ly adverb   _____ (6 pts)

☐ ☐ ☐ _who–which_ clause   _____ (6 pts)

☐ ☐ ☐ strong verb   _____ (6 pts)

☐ ☐ ☐ because clause   _____ (6 pts)

☐ ☐ ☐ quality adjective   _____ (6 pts)

Decorations (Use at least one per para.) ("dec" in margin or italics)   **(2 pts each)**

☐ alliteration   _____ (2 pts)

☐ simile   _____ (2 pts)

☐ 3sss   _____ (2 pts)

MECHANICS

☐ banned words: go/went say/said nice/mean   _____ (-1 pt)

MORE ADVANCED ADDITIONS

☐ vocabulary words (_Label voc or bold._)   _____

☐ conversation   _____

☐ dual adjective, verb, or -ly adverb   _____

☐ triple extension   _____

Total _____/50

Custom total _____ / _____

Unit 5: Writing from Pictures

Teachers, review Unit 6: Summarizing Multiple References in the TWSS workbook before teaching Lessons 18–21. If you have the seminar on DVD, watch the corresponding lesson.

Unit 6: Summarizing Multiple References

Lesson 18: Medieval Cathedrals

Review
Allow time for some students to read their stories from Lesson 17.

Multiple Source Research Reports
When you are asked to write a *research* report, your teacher will require that you use several sources from which to gather facts. The IEW method for note taking and outlining will help you to do this successfully. In this lesson you will write a 1-paragraph report, but you will have more than one source text. This means you will first take notes from each source; then, you will pick and choose the notes you would like to put into a key word outline from which you will write the paragraph. Follow these steps:

Day 1

1. Read Source 1, "Grandiose Structures." On your own paper, formatted like page 122, write three key words to help you remember each of the facts you think are the most interesting or most important.

Instruct students to take out a clean sheet of paper and format it like page 122. This is the paper they will take notes on.

---

2. Repeat Step 1 with Source 2, "Awe-Inspiring Cathedrals." Do not note facts that you already noted from the first source.

3. Once you have notes from both sources, choose five to seven that are interesting or important, and organize them into one fused outline on page 123. Remember that report paragraphs need topic sentences. Notice that *cathedrals* has been filled in on the topic sentence line. What main idea about cathedrals would make a good topic sentence?

Let students offer ideas. Choose one to put on the sample fused outline on the whiteboard.

---

4. To make a fused outline, under the topic sentence write no more than seven facts from your notes. Arrange the notes in an order that makes sense.

Teachers, do this with the students. Put ideas on a whiteboard. Let them copy into their books. However, if they would like to choose different facts from those that you put on the board, that is okay.

---

5. Use the fused outline to tell back, in complete sentences, the ideas you will include in your paragraph.

6. Study page 124 to learn a new dress-up: the www.asia clause.

Days 2–4

1. Polish the "Magic Lamp" story from Lesson 16.

2. Use your fused outline (not your notes) to write a paragraph. Follow the checklist.

3. Cut out and learn the vocabulary words for Lesson 18. Review all.

Literature Suggestion

With Lessons 18–19 read *Otto of the Silver Hand* by Howard Pyle.

Unit 6: Summarizing Multiple References

Source Text 1

Grandiose Structures

A prominent symbol of the Middle Ages is the cathedral. Cathedrals symbolize the importance of religion and the power of the church during that time. They are large churches that served as the headquarters of a bishop. In fact, the word *cathedral* comes from a Greek word that means seat because the bishop's seat or throne was inside the cathedral. Between 1000 and 1540, hundreds of huge cathedrals were built all across Europe. Each was a monumental undertaking that required hundreds of workers and over one hundred years to complete. They were larger than castles, and far more glorious. Cathedrals were often built in the shape of a cross with very high ceilings, and they were filled with awe-inspiring art and architecture. Cathedrals were used for daily church services, religious ceremonies, and public meetings. A city's public life centered around its cathedral. These grandiose structures reminded the people of the power and authority of the church and the glory of God.

    Institute for Excellence in Writing

Sample KWO (Students will write on their own paper.)

I. _symb. M-A, show, power, church_

1. _lg, churches, HQ, bishop_

2. _1000–1540, 100s, built, Eur_

3. _100s workers, 100s yrs_

4. _> castles, >glorious_

5. _w/☺ art, architecture_

6. _@ center, city's, pub life_

Source Text 2

Awe-Inspiring Cathedrals

During the Middle Ages enormous and splendid churches were erected to inspire people to faith.
These churches were called cathedrals. The cathedrals were the largest structures in cities. They
were built for the glory of God. They impressed upon the people the power and majesty of God.
They were built from millions of pounds of carved stones. They were adorned with magnificent
sculptures, paintings, tapestries, murals, and stained glass windows. These works of art often
depicted scenes and events from the Bible or from church history to help peasants who could not
read remember them. Since the cathedral was for the glory of God, everything in it, including
seemingly insignificant things such as doorknobs and hinges, had to be beautiful. Building a
cathedral took the efforts and money of an entire community and could take centuries to build.
People who began work on a cathedral knew they would not see it finished in their lifetime.
Cities took great pride in their cathedrals and often competed with other cities to have the tallest
spire. The building of the cathedrals helped advance art and architecture in an otherwise dark
time. Today hundreds of medieval cathedrals across Europe continue to awe visitors.

Taking notes will be easier if you write them on a separate sheet of paper rather than below because you can put your paper next to the source text.

Key Word Outline - Medieval Cathedrals

Source 1: "Grandiose Structures"

I. _symb. M-A, show, power, church_

1. _lg, churches, HQ, bishop_

2. _1000–1540, 100s, built, Eur_

3. _100s workers, 100s yrs_

4. _> castles, >glorious_

5. _w/☺ art, architecture_

6. _@ center, city's, pub life_

Source 2: "Awe-Inspiring Cathedrals"

I. _inspire, ppl, faith_

1. _4, glory, God_

2. _millions, carved, stones_

3. _embell w/sculpt, pntg, tapestries, windows_

4. _ppl began, ⊘ ⊙ ⊙, finished_

5. _city, > pride, compete w/_

6. _helped, adv, art, arch, Dark Ages_

Fused Outline - Medieval Cathedrals

I. (Topic): cathedrals, *symb, power, Church, M-A*

1. *1000–1540, 100s built, inspire, faith, ppl*

2. *took, 100s workers, 100s yrs*

3. *millions, carved, stones*

4. *lgest, structures, > castles, > glorious*

5. *embell w/sculpt, pntg, tapestries, windows*

6. *@ center, pub, life*

7. *advanced, art, Dk Ages*

Clincher

www.asia Clause

You have been using the *who-which* and the *because* clauses for a while. Now you will learn to form the same type of clause with other words. This acronym will help you remember them: www.asia. Each letter is the first letter of one of the words that can begin a clausal dress-up:

---

when, while, where, as, since, if, although

A www.asia clause helps you add more detail to a sentence. Memorize these words. You can also find them near the beginning of the SRN.

Example: Cathedrals were enormous churches <u>where</u> a bishop had his official seat of teaching authority.

A sentence with one of the www.asia words must contain two clauses, each with its own subject and verb. This is because the www.asia word will turn a sentence it is placed in front of into an incomplete thought (dependent clause).

Always check that a sentence with this dress-up is composed of two sentences plus the www.asia word. In the sample above, if you remove the word *where*, you will see two sentences. What are they?

Remember, too, that a comma must follow the entire www.asia clause unless it is at the end of a sentence where a period will replace the comma. Usually, do not place a comma in front of a www.asia clause. Indicate this dress-up by underlining the www.asia word.

Finish each sentence by using a different www.asia word to begin a clause.

Since they wanted to glorify God,
Although they might not see it completed,

1.   *When they were able,*_____, the people of a city worked

together on their cathedral.

2.   The people of a city took great pride in their cathedral _____

_____*when it was finally finished since it represented decades of hard work*_____ .

Lesson 18 Checklist - Medieval Cathedrals

FORMAT

☐ Modified MLA format (See Appendix 1.) _____ (3 pts)

STRUCTURE

☐ Topic sentence with key words highlighted _____ (3 pts)

☐ Clincher with key words highlighted _____ (3 pts)

☐ Title repeats or reflects key words from final clincher. _____ (3 pts)

STYLE Each paragraph must contain at least one of each element of style.

¶ 1 Dress-Ups (Underline one of each; abbreviate in right margin.) **(3 pts each)**

☐ -ly adverb _____ (3 pts)

☐ *who–which* clause _____ (3 pts)

☐ strong verb _____ (3 pts)

☐ because clause _____ (3 pts)

☐ quality adjective _____ (3 pts)

☐ www.asia clause _____ (3 pts)

Decorations (Use one anywhere.) ("dec" in margin or italics) **(2 pts each)**

☐ alliteration, simile, or 3sss _____ (2 pts)

MECHANICS

☐ banned words: go/went say/said nice/mean _____ (-1 pt)

MORE ADVANCED ADDITIONS

☐ vocabulary words (*Label voc or bold.*) _____

☐ dual adjective, verb, or -ly adverb _____

☐ triple extension _____

Total _____ /32

Custom total _____ / _____

A Squire Arming a Knight

Unit 6: Summarizing Multiple References

Lesson 19: Knights, Part 1

Review

1. What is a fused outline?

an outline made from notes from multiple sources

2. What must a fused outline begin with?

It must begin with a topic sentence idea.

In Lessons 19–20, you are going to again use more than one source of information to help you write a report. This time you will write a 3-paragraph report. On pages 128–132 there are three different articles about knights. You are going to choose some of the information in these articles and use it to write your report, one paragraph at a time.

The Assignment

Day 1

1. Before you begin taking notes, you must know the topics of each of your paragraphs. To choose your topics, first scan the paragraphs in each source to determine the topics covered in them. Looking at the first and last sentence of each paragraph should give you a good clue.

2. Choose only three of the topics for your report. Choose topics that are covered in two of the sources. Include *the duties of knights* as the first topic.

3. Write each topic at the top of its own sheet of paper formatted like page 133.

Help students prepare and format their note-taking pages.

4. Take key word notes for *the first topic only* (duties of knights). Write the notes from all sources for this topic on your first piece of paper by reading *only the paragraphs about knights' duties.*

If students desire to choose "knights of the Crusades," they will need to find another source of their own.

5. Once you have notes from the sources that cover your topic, organize them into one fused outline. Use page 134. Begin with words for a topic sentence. Then choose the most interesting or important facts from your notes that you want in your paragraph, and write them in an order that makes sense.

Days 2–4

1. Polish the King and the Dragon story from Lesson 17.

2. Use the fused outline on page 134 to write ONE paragraph about knights' duties. Use the checklist after the outline. Attach it to your paragraph.

3. Cut out and learn new vocabulary words. Continue to review and use previous words.

Point out to students that in Source Text 1 on this page, the topic sentence of the first paragraph is the third sentence. The first two sentences are introductory sentences.

Unit 6: Summarizing Multiple References

Source Text 1

If you will add a bibliography, pretend this an article from the 2000 edition of *Verstegen's Encyclopedia of the Middle Ages*.

Knights

Topic: origin of term "knight"

When you think of the Middle Ages, do knights come to mind? Knights were the armored, horse-mounted soldiers of the Middle Ages. There are two explanations for the origin of the term. The first says that it comes from the Anglo-Saxon word for boy: *cniht*, because the early knights were not much more than boys hired to serve a nobleman. The other explanation says the term comes from the Old English word *cnight*, which means household retainer. This is what the English called the Norman soldiers of William the Conqueror who were in their land to squash revolts against the new king.

Topic: duties

Knights had many duties in service to the lords they pledged to serve. They were first and foremost soldiers. They protected their lord's land from invaders. Often they went off to battle for their lord. In exchange, they were given large amounts of land. When not in battle, they kept law and order in the land and managed the affairs of the estate. Knights also practiced a variety of combat skills like jousting, hand-to-hand combat, and archery in tournaments. Hundreds of knights would come together for such tournaments, which kept them fit and provided great entertainment for the people. Knights were loyal, well-trained, respected soldiers.

Institute for Excellence in Writing

Topic: Code of Chivalry

Knights followed the Code of Chivalry. At that time, *chivalry* meant "horse soldiers." Because these soldiers all agreed to live by the same code, *chivalry* became the word used to describe the behavior and ethics of the knights. Above all else, knights were supposed to love and protect the church and its teachings, honor their lord, and fight for their country. They were also supposed to protect women and the feeble. If they fell in love with a lady, they had to do any task she gave them to do. Loyalty, courtesy, courage, and honor were the main virtues the code expected in all knights.

Topic: armor

Knights would not be knights without their shining armor. Early armor was made of chain mail, but that only stopped simple arrows, not crossbow arrows or sword blows. So blacksmiths made metal plates to put over the chain mail. Over the years the armor improved and became more decorated. It became very expensive. One suit in Germany cost the equivalent of what a modern tank would cost us today.

Topic: knights of Crusades

The most famous knights were the knights of the Crusades. These were the knights who traveled to Jerusalem and the Middle East to recapture the Christian holy lands invaded by Muslims. These knights also hoped to gain land for themselves. The first crusade was the most successful—it recaptured Jerusalem in 1099, but not for long. For the next two hundred years, Christian knights fought Muslims for control of Jerusalem, and power changed hands many times. But in 1244, Muslims conquered and retained it for the rest of the Middle Ages.

Source Text 2

If you will add a bibliography, pretend this is a book published by ABC Publishers of New York in 2006.

The Age of Knights
by Jane Doe

Topic: soldiers (duty)

"The Age of Knights" began in about A.D. 900 and lasted until the 1500s. The knight's main duty was to serve as the most elite of the soldiers for his lord. The other soldiers were archers and foot soldiers. On the battlefield knights were like the tanks of today. They were clad in armor and rode horses that were also covered in armor. They could plow through ranks of foot soldiers. Knights were also the wealthiest soldiers. For their services they were usually paid a large amount of land. This was necessary for them to be able to raise enough money for their horses and armor, which were very expensive. A war horse could cost as much as a small airplane would cost today. Knights, therefore, were part of a wealthy, elite class of warriors.

Topic: Code of Chivalry

People of the Middle Ages believed knighthood was a holy calling, so knights were bound by the Code of Chivalry. This was a set of standards that controlled their behavior. In war, a chivalrous knight was to be brave, loyal to his lord, and willing to sacrifice himself for the greater good. At home, a knight promised to defend the weak, to serve God and his king at all times, and never to boast. Toward noble ladies, he was to be gracious and gentle. But in reality, these standards were not always followed. Many knights broke rules to gain power or wealth. Some even became "robber knights" and turned to organized crime. Others plundered villages. Still, knighthood is known for the ideal of the Code of Chivalry.

Topic: armor

Knighthood is also known for the armor knights wore. Early armor was made of chain mail—thousands of tiny metal rings woven together. But when the crossbow was invented, chain mail did not protect knights well enough. So a suit of metal plates was invented. It became so complicated that it took two men to put it on a knight. It was so cumbersome that if a knight was knocked from his horse, it was very difficult for him to fight. The main weapon of a knight was his sword. It could be twice as long as his arm and weigh as much as a bicycle. A knight's armor was expensive, hot, and heavy!

Topic: training

Training for knighthood began at age seven. Boys this young were called pages. They learned to ride and care for horses, fight with a sword, wrestle, and hunt with a falcon. They also played games like chess to learn battle strategies. At around 12–15, a page could become a squire. As a squire, he served under one knight. He took care of the knight's armor, weapons, and horses. Sometimes he even followed him into battle. He was also the only one allowed to help his master in a tournament. At as early as age 16, a squire could be knighted by a knight. Sometimes this happened on the battlefield, but usually it was a formal ceremony. The squire would kneel before the knight. The knight would then tap his shoulder with his sword and say, "I dub you knight."

Topic: knights today

Today in many countries like England, there are still knights. But they do not ride horses and wear shining armor. Instead, knighthood is an honor bestowed on someone who does something outstanding for his country. A knight today is given the title "Sir" if he is a man. But a woman can be knighted, too. A female knight is called "Dame." But this knighthood is very different from the knighthood of the Middle Ages.

Unit 6: Summarizing Multiple References

Source Text 3

If you will add a bibliography, pretend this is an article by Lori Verstegen on the website called *Medieval Highlights*, posted in May 2015.

Becoming a Knight

Topic: who

Many boys of the Middle Ages probably dreamed of becoming knights. While technically anyone could become a knight by proving himself in battle, knighthood was generally only for the wealthy, noble class. That is because a knight's armor, weapons, and horses were extremely expensive.

Topic: page

When a nobleman decided his son was to be a knight, the boy was sent to live with a knight as one of his pages when he was about seven years old. At this stage the boy was a servant to the knight and learned proper behavior and good manners. Pages also studied the arts, music, and battle strategies. It was basically like being in school, with the teacher being the knight's squire. Eventually pages would practice sword fighting with wooden swords and shields and horseback riding with lances.

Topic: squire

At around fifteen years old, after fighting skills were proficient, a page advanced to squire, which means "shield bearer." A squire cared for his knight's horses, cleaned his armor and weapons, and followed him into battle. Squires continued to practice their fighting skills with real weapons and by jousting. Young men were usually squires for five or six years.

Topic: dubbing

Once a squire proved his skill and bravery in battle, he could become a knight in a ceremony called a dubbing. He was to spend the entire night before the dubbing alone in prayer. At the ceremony the squire knelt in front of the king or knight, who then tapped him on the shoulder with his sword. The new knight would take an oath to honor and protect the king and the church.

These sample notes are for Topic A only. Students will do similarly for Topics B or C in Lesson 20.

Key Word Outlines

Take notes on your own paper, following this format. Each topic for Lessons 19–20 needs its own paper.

Topic A: Duties of knights

Source 1: "Knights" (quotation marks because it is an article)

I.   > duties, to , lords

1.   1st, soldiers

2.   protect, land, invaders

3.   → battles, paid, w/land

4.   ⊘ battles, law, & order

5.   + pract, combat, skills, tournaments

6.   loyal, respected

Source 2: *The Age of Knights* by Doe (italics because it is a book)

I.   1 kind, soldier

1.   like, tanks, w/armor

2.   + horse, w/armor

3.   plow, foot, soldiers

4. $$, elite, class

5.   _____

Source 3: "Becoming a Knight" by Verstegen
   (**Note:** *This source will be used only for a paragraph about knights' training.*)

I.   This source text does not have information for Topic A.

1.   _____

2.   _____

3.   _____

4.   _____

Fused Outline - Duties of Knights

I. Topic A: *knights, > duties, lords*

  1.   *1st, soldiers, protect, land*

  2.   *often, ➜ battle*

  3.   *lk, tanks, w/armor, + horses*

  4.   *plow, foot, soldiers*

  5.   *⊘ battle, law, & order*

  6.   *+ pract, combat, skills, tournaments*

Clincher A

Lesson 19 Rough Checklist Topic A - Knights: Duties

FORMAT

- [ ] Modified MLA format (See Appendix 1.) _____ (2 pts)

STRUCTURE

- [ ] Topic sentence with key words highlighted _____ (5 pts)
- [ ] Clincher with key words highlighted _____ (3 pts)
- [ ] (no title yet)

STYLE Each paragraph must contain at least one of each element of style.

¶ 1 Dress-Ups (Underline one of each; abbreviate in right margin.)   **(3 pts each)**

- [ ] -ly adverb _____ (3 pts)
- [ ] who-which clause _____ (3 pts)
- [ ] strong verb _____ (3 pts)
- [ ] because clause _____ (3 pts)
- [ ] quality adjective _____ (3 pts)
- [ ] www.asia clause _____ (3 pts)

Decoration (Use one anywhere.) ("dec" in margin or italics)   **(2 pts each)**

- [ ] alliteration, simile, or 3sss _____ (2 pts)

MECHANICS

- [ ] banned words: go/went say/said nice/mean _____ (-1 pt)

MORE ADVANCED ADDITIONS

- [ ] vocabulary words (*Label voc or bold.*) _____
- [ ] dual adjective, verb, or -ly adverb _____
- [ ] triple extension _____

Total _____/30

Custom total _____ / _____

Unit 6: Summarizing Multiple References

Institute for Excellence in Writing

Do not collect the Topic A paragraph from Lesson 19. Instead, have students read their topic sentences and clinchers. Have a few students read their entire paragraph.

Unit 6: Summarizing Multiple References

Lesson 20: Knights, Part 2

Review

1. What did you look at to write your paragraph about knights' duties?   *the fused outline*

2. Read the topic sentence and clincher of your paragraph. Did you remember to highlight the key words that tell the topic?

Sentence Openers

Thus far, you have learned most of the IEW dress-ups and some of the decorations. In this lesson you will learn a different kind of element of style. To help you appreciate it, read the following two versions of part of a report. What is the difference between them? Which sounds better?

> **Version 1**
>
> Knights of the Middle Ages had many duties. They were soldiers. They fought for their lords. They wore shining armor. There were not always battles. Knights practiced their skills in tournaments. They kept order in the land. They rescued fair ladies from villains. Knights were very busy.
>
> **Version 2**
>
> Knights of the Middle Ages had many duties. First and foremost, they were soldiers who fought bravely for their lords. In battle, they wore the shining armor they are famous for. When there were no battles to fight, knights practiced their skills in tournaments. They also kept order in the land. Additionally, they rescued fair ladies from villains. With so many tasks, knights were very busy.

In the paragraphs above, you should have noticed that in Version 1, all the sentences begin with the subject and are about the same length. This makes writing boring!

One way to make your writing more sophisticated is to begin some of your sentences with something other than the subject and to use sentences of differing lengths—some short, medium, and long. Can you see how Version 2 accomplished both of these things?

In this lesson you will learn one special kind of sentence that will help you begin a sentence with something other than the subject of the sentence. So that you can indicate it when you use it, it is given a number. (You will learn more sentence openers later that will be given other numbers.)

Be sure students place a 2 in the left margin across from the lines that include the #2 openers. Note: Students who type their work may prefer to place a [2] directly in front of the #2 sentence as in the student samples. This is acceptable as well. See pages 238–239.

#2 Sentence Opener: A Prepositional Phrase

The #2 sentence begins with a prepositional phrase: **preposition + noun (no verb)**.

There is a list of prepositions in the SRN. Turn there. This week, try to memorize as many as you can. Until you have them memorized, you may refer to that list. Here are the two #2 sentences in Version 2 of the knight paragraph. Indicate them by placing a 2 in the left margin.

2   In battle, they wore the shining armor they are famous for.

2   With so many tasks, knights were very busy.

Note that the preposition begins a phrase placed in front of a complete sentence. This is the structure of a #2 sentence. If your prepositional phrase has five words or more, follow it with a comma. A comma is optional with shorter phrases.

Label the #2 sentences in the knight paragraph (Version 2) on page 137.

Practice

Take out the paragraph you wrote last week (duties of knights). Find a place where you can add a #2 sentence opener. Remember to put a *2* in the left margin next to it. Share your idea with the class.

You will practice more with sentences about knights on page 141.

    Institute for Excellence in Writing

To teach prepositions, I tell students that these words show a relationship between one object and another. Then, on the whiteboard I draw two rabbits (Mr. and Mrs.) spaced apart, some trees, and a rock with a hole in it. I let students look at the list of prepositions and tell me, using sentences that begin with one, how Mr. Rabbit relates to other things. Have fun with it. (It is okay if students use things not in the picture.)

(Examples: By the rock Mr. R. sits. Over the rock Mr. R. jumps. In the rock Mr. R. hides. Without Mrs. R. Mr. R. is sad. With Mrs. R. Mr. R. is happy. From the forest he hops. To Mrs. R. he hops. Through the forest ... In the river ... During the day ...

The Assignment

Day 1

1. From the sources on pages 128–132, take key word notes for *Topic B only*. (This will likely be armor, Code of Chivalry, or training.) Write the notes on your own paper, formatted like page 133. Take notes by reading *only the paragraphs about your topic*. Only two of the sources will have information you can use.

   In a class, if all students have chosen the same topic, you may take notes together. If not, students may work in groups with teacher supervision.

If students are comfortable with note taking, after you help them format their paper like page 133, assign the note taking for homework. Spend class time on the #2 sentence opener and bibliography.

2. Once you have notes from both sources, organize them into one fused outline. Use page 140. Begin with words for a topic sentence. Then choose the facts from your notes that you want in your paragraph, and write them in an order that makes sense.

3. Use page 141 to brainstorm ideas for using sentence openers and to learn how to do a bibliography.

Days 2–4

1. Polish the Cathedrals paragraph from Lesson 18.

2. Use the *fused* outline on page 140 to write *one* paragraph about your second topic. Add it to the first paragraph (Topic A from Lesson 19). Follow the checklist on page 142. Remember to add the #2 sentence opener to both paragraphs.

   Note: We will add introduction and conclusion paragraphs in a later lesson. For now, begin and end each paragraph with a topic sentence and clincher for only the topic of the paragraph. Do not lose your paragraphs after they are returned!

3. Repeat the process for your third topic: Take notes from at least two sources, and fuse the notes on page 140. Use the fused outline to write a third paragraph.

4. Put all three paragraphs into one report. Attach the checklist on page 142.

5. Add a bibliography. See page 141.

6. Cut out and learn vocabulary words for Lesson 20. Review previous.

Literature Suggestion:

With Lessons 20–23 read *Robin Hood*. There are many versions to choose from. The Dover Evergreen Classic by J. Walker McFadden is one possibility.

(Use these outlines only after you have taken notes from the sources on pages 128–132 on your own paper, formatted like page 133.)

Fused Outline: Topic B

II. Topic B: _Notes and outlines will vary depending on topics chosen._

1. _____

2. _____

3. _____

4. _____

5. _____

Clincher B

Fused Outline: Topic C

III. Topic C: _Notes and outlines will vary depending on topics chosen._

1. _____

2. _____

3. _____

4. _____

5. _____

Clincher C

Brainstorming Elements of Style

#2 Sentence Ideas (Prepositional Phrases)

In battle
1. _____*With thick iron plates*_____ armor protected knights.

At all times
2. _____*With all his heart and strength,*_____ a knight was supposed to protect the church.

At a young age
3. _____*With hopes of knighthood*_____ boys left home to train.

Bibliography

A bibliography is a list of the sources that were used to write a research report. It is placed as the last page of the report. See the SRN for instructions on how to format a bibliography. Use the information under the title of each source text on pages 128–132 to list sources from this book. If you used some of your own sources, include those as well. Internet articles can be tricky to list. Here is how to format an Internet article listing:

Author's last name, first name. [If no author given, just skip this.] "Title of Article." [in quotes]

Title of website. [in italics] Publisher or Sponsor. [Put n.p. if not given.] Date posted.

[n.d. if not given.] Web. Date you looked at the site.

If time permits, help students with the bibliography. As they use the SRN, let them dictate to you. Here are the answers:

Bibliography

Doe, Jane. *The Age of Knights.* New York: ABC Publishers, 2006. Print.

"Knights." *Verstegen's Encyclopedia of the Middle Ages.* 2000 ed. Print.

Verstegen, Lori. "Becoming a Knight." *Medieval Highlights.* n.p. May 2015. Web. [Add the day month year you read the article.]

In Lesson 25, students will add a paragraph of introduction and a paragraph of conclusion to their knights paragraphs. Tell them to be sure to save their paragraphs when they are returned.

Unit 6: Summarizing Multiple References

Lesson 20 Final Checklist (Body) - Knights

FORMAT

☐ Modified MLA format (See Appendix 1.) _____ (2 pts)

STRUCTURE

☐ Topic sentences with key words highlighted, each paragraph _____ (5 pts)

☐ Clinchers with key words highlighted, each paragraph _____ (5 pts)

☐ (No title yet)

STYLE Each paragraph must contain at least one of each element of style.

¶ 1	¶ 2	¶ 3	Dress-Ups (Underline one of each; abbreviate in right margin.)	(2 pts each)	
☐	☐	☐	-ly adverb	_____ (6 pts)	
☐	☐	☐	*who-which* clause	_____ (6 pts)	
☐	☐	☐	strong verb	_____ (6 pts)	
☐	☐	☐	because clause	_____ (6 pts)	
☐	☐	☐	quality adjective	_____ (6 pts)	
☐	☐	☐	www.asia clause	_____ (6 pts)	

Decorations (Use at least one per para.) ("dec" in margin or italics) (2 pts each)

☐	☐	☐	alliteration, simile, or 3sss	_____ (6 pts)

Sentence Openers (numbered; one of each as possible) (2 pts each)

☐	☐	☐	[2] prepositional	_____ (6 pts)

MECHANICS

☐ banned words: go/went say/said nice/mean _____ (-1 pt)

☐ bibliography _____ (10 pts)

MORE ADVANCED ADDITIONS

☐ vocabulary words (*Label voc or bold.*) _____

☐ dual adjective, verb, or -ly adverb _____

☐ triple extension _____

Total _____/70

Custom total _____ / _____

Lesson 21: King Richard and His Brother John

Unit 6: Summarizing Multiple References

Lesson 21: King Richard and His Brother John

Review

Read a #2 sentence from your knights report. Play Preposition Round Robin.

Preposition Round Robin

Give students one minute to study the prepositions listed in the SRN. Then, have them all stand up. In turn, each student has ten seconds to name a preposition. You write them on the whiteboard. If a student gives a preposition, he gets a ticket and remains standing. If a student is unable to name one, he must sit down. If he gives a word that is not a preposition, he must sit down. If he gives a preposition already on the whiteboard, he must sit down. Continue until one student is left standing. If you get down to two or three students, and none can give you a preposition, they tie for the win. Winner gets five extra tickets.

This assignment will provide more practice with note taking from multiple sources and will add library (or Internet) research. It is one of the more difficult assignments. Teachers of young students may opt to omit this lesson.

You will follow the same procedure taught in previous Unit 6 lessons to write a research paper about King Richard and his brother King John. One source is provided for you. You must find one or two other sources of your own from either the library or the Internet.

Important: Choose short and simple sources. History textbooks, Internet articles (especially those googled "for kids"), encyclopedia articles, and short children's books will make the best sources.

The difficulty of this lesson will be determined largely upon the level of difficulty of the sources you find. Parents or teachers should strive to help students find short, simple sources. If you go to the library, ask the librarian for help. Learning to use the library is a valuable skill in and of itself.

Each paragraph needs a topic. The report needs two body paragraphs:

    A. King Richard

    B. King John

Because this is a 2-paragraph report and we will not be adding a paragraph of introduction or conclusion, you will need to add an introductory sentence and final clincher to tie the entire report together (as you did for your Charlemagne report). If you simply begin with the topic sentence for King Richard, your reader will expect the entire report to be about him. You must begin by letting your reader know the subject of the entire report, so begin by mentioning both Richard and John. Why are they together in the same report? How are they related?

Notice how the source text begins and ends.

Unit 6: Summarizing Multiple References

The Assignment

Day 1

1. In class, using the source provided, take notes for each of the topics. Be sure to use a separate paper for each topic you will write about, with room for notes from one or two additional sources on each paper.

   Format your papers like page 147.

Help students prepare and format their note taking pages.

2. Brainstorm ideas for including a #2 sentence opener. Even though you have not made a fused outline yet, write the ideas for #2 sentences at the bottom of each fused outline page (pages 148–149).

3. As a class, brainstorm ideas for an introductory sentence and final clincher. What can you say about both Richard and John? Why are they in the same report? These sentences will tie your entire report together like topic sentences and clinchers tie paragraphs together.

Days 2–4

1. For each topic, one at a time, take notes from one or two additional sources of your own. Add these notes to the pages you began in class.

2. From your notes for each topic, make a fused outline as you did in Lessons 18–20. Use pages 148–149 or your own paper formatted like these pages.

3. Remember to add an introductory sentence before Topic Sentence A. Mention both Richard and John.

4. Write your paragraphs from your fused outlines. Follow and attach the checklist on page 150.

5. Add a bibliography. See page 141 for help with Internet articles. To list the source in this book, see the "Bibliography Entry" that follows it. For all other entries, see the SRN section on Bibliography/Works Cited.

   There are no new vocabulary words for this lesson.

Source Text

King Richard and His Brother John

If you have seen Walt Disney's *Robin Hood* or read any of the stories about Robin Hood, you

have heard of King Richard and his evil brother, Prince John. They were sons of King Henry II,

and each ruled England for a short time. Richard I was the king of England from 1189–1199. He

was called "Coeur de Lion," meaning lionhearted, because he was valiant in battle. Richard was

loved by the people of England, and he was thought of as a hero. However, he was rarely in his

country. He actually spent less than one year out of the ten that he was king in England. Instead,

he was off fighting battles, like the Third Crusade to recapture the Holy Land in Palestine. He did

not win this crusade, but he was able to make a truce with the Muslim leader Saladin. This truce

allowed Christians to go to Jerusalem. While King Richard was away, John tried to rule in his

place, but he was greedy and was not liked by the people. He was not like his brother, Richard.

But in 1199, Richard was killed in a battle in France, so John became king.

John, like his brother, had a nickname, but it was not because he was brave. John was

not a proficient warrior or leader. The people did not expect him to inherit much land, so John

was called John Lackland. This was probably a name he hated. When he became king, he was

a selfish, greedy king. He was also a poor warrior and lost England's land in France. This made

the nobles (called barons) angry because they lost their wealth there. To pay for his losses, John

raised the taxes on the people, which made them even angrier. The barons fought for power.

Eventually, in 1215, they forced King John to sign a document called the Magna Carta (Great

Charter). This charter required the king to obey the same laws as his subjects. Under the Magna

Carta, the law controlled the king, not the king the law, as John preferred. It also gave the people

some rights. Soon John tried to go back on the Magna Carta, but the barons then declared war

on him. Shortly thereafter he died, and his son Henry III became king. So both Richard and John

had fairly short reigns over England.

Bibliography

Verstegen, Lori. "King Richard and His Brother John." *Medieval History-Based Writing Lessons.*

Locust Grove: Institute for Excellence in Writing, 2015. 145–146. Print.

Key Word Outlines

For each topic of your report, take notes on your own paper formatted like this. Be sure to have a separate notes page for each of your topics.

Topic __A__ : *King Richard* _____

Source 1: "King Richard and His Brother" (Verstegen)

1. _*king, Eng, 1189–1199*_____

2. _*"the lionhearted" b/c, valiant*_____

3. _*ppl, loved, but, away*_____

4. _*→, 3rd Crusade, Saladin*_____

5. _*⊘ capt, Jeru, truce*_____

6. _*→, France, XX*_____

Source 2:

1. _*Sources 2 and 3 will be sources students have*_

2. _*found from the library or at home.*_____

3. _____

4. _____

5. _____

6. _____

Source 3: (optional)

1. _____

2. _____

3. _____

4. _____

5. _____

6. _____

This will be on a different paper from Topic A. It is for Topic B, under Source 1.

II. *Topic B:* _*King John*_____

1. _*after, Richard, John, ♔*_____

2. _*⊘ prof, war, leader*_____

3. _*lost, Eng, land, France*_____

4. _*barons, angry, b/c, ↓ $$*_____

5. _*1215, forced, Magna Carta*_____

6. _*♔, subj, laws, ppl, ↑ rights*_____

7. _*1st, written, Constitution*_____

Unit 6: Summarizing Multiple References

Fused Outline: Topic A

Fill out this outline using the notes you took from two or three sources for Topic A: King Richard.

Introductory sentence: *Richard and John were brothers who ruled England differently.*

(Write something about both Richard and John to introduce the entire report. How are they related? Why are they in the same report?)

I. Topic A: _____

1. _____

2. _____

3. _____

4. _____

5. _____

6. _____

7. _____

Clincher A *(Reflect the topic sentence for King Richard, not the introductory sentence.)*

#2 Prepositional Sentence Opener Idea

During the Third Crusade King Richard hoped to recapture Jerusalem.

Fused Outline: Topic B

Fill out this outline using notes you took from two or three sources for Topic B: King John.

II.   Topic B: _____

    1. _____

    2. _____

    3. _____

    4. _____

    5. _____

    6. _____

    7. _____

    Clincher B

    Final clincher *(End by reflecting the introductory sentence about both Richard and John.)*

#2 Prepositional Sentence Opener Idea

With his brother away, Prince John could rule as he pleased. _____

Unit 6: Summarizing Multiple References

Lesson 21 Final Checklist -
King Richard and His Brother John

FORMAT

☐ Modified MLA format (See Appendix 1.) _____ (2 pts)

STRUCTURE

☐ Topic sentences with key words highlighted, each paragraph _____ (6 pts)

☐ Clinchers with key words highlighted, each paragraph _____ (4 pts)

☐ Title repeats or reflects key words from final clincher. _____ (3 pts)

☐ Introductory sentence _____ (5 pts)

☐ Final clincher _____ (3 pts)

STYLE Each paragraph must contain at least one of each element of style.

¶ 1   ¶ 2 Dress-Ups (Underline one of each; abbreviate in right margin.)   **(2 pts each)**

☐ ☐ -ly adverb _____ (4 pts)

☐ ☐ who-which clause _____ (4 pts)

☐ ☐ strong verb _____ (4 pts)

☐ ☐ because clause _____ (4 pts)

☐ ☐ quality adjective _____ (4 pts)

☐ ☐ www.asia clause _____ (4 pts)

Decorations (Use at least one per para.) ("dec" in margin or italics)   **(2 pts each)**

☐ ☐ alliteration, simile, 3sss _____ (4 pts)

Sentence Opener (numbered; one of each as possible)   **(2 pts each)**

☐ ☐ [2] prepositional _____ (4 pts)

MECHANICS

☐ banned words: go/went say/said nice/mean _____ (-1 pt)

☐ bibliography _____ (5 pts)

MORE ADVANCED ADDITIONS

☐ vocabulary words (*Label voc or bold.*) _____

☐ dual adjective, verb, or -ly adverb _____

☐ triple extension _____

Total _____/60

Custom total _____ / _____

Teachers, review Unit 7: Inventive Writing in the TWSS workbook before teaching Lessons 22–24. If you have the seminar on DVD, watch the corresponding lesson.

Unit 7: Inventive Writing

Lesson 22: Favorite Amusements, Part 1

Review

Play the sentence stretching game from the TM.

Follow page 275, using the elements of style you have taught thus far. Also require a vocabulary word in each sentence because there is a vocabulary quiz next week. (Or you could play a vocabulary game.)

Notes from the Brain

In the following lessons, you are going to write paragraphs with the help of source texts, but you will still need to make a key word outline to organize your ideas. So, where are you going to get your notes? You are going to get them from your brain! To do so, you must learn to ask yourself questions. Memorizing some question starter words and phrases will help you.

Who?   What?   When?   Where?   Why?   How? **How feel?   Best thing?   Worst thing?**

You will practice using these questions to help give you ideas for what to write in response to the prompt below.

Prompt

The main entertainment and fun during medieval times was in the form of feasts, fairs, and festivals. Most villages had one each month, and they were often associated with religious holidays or events. They were fun days filled with food, music, and dancing. There were entertainers like jugglers, musicians, acrobats, and storytellers. There were competitions like archery, hammer throwing, jousting, and wrestling. Everyone looked forward to these fun-filled days.

Entertainment today is a bit different. We have access to many different kinds of amusements almost any day of the year.

Write two paragraphs about your favorite amusement, entertainment, or holiday.

You may write about two kinds of entertainment you enjoy, like amusement parks, movies, sporting events, books, concerts, games, holidays, or the like. Or, you could choose one subject and write about two things you like about it. (For example, if you choose amusement parks, you could write about two different rides.)

Unit 7: Inventive Writing

The Assignment

Day 1

1. Since you need two paragraphs, you need two topics to write about. As a class, list several possible subjects with topics to match.

2. The teacher should model the question process by choosing one of the subjects and its two topics to outline together. She should ask questions and encourage specific details and examples. Students should not copy the class KWO, but they should notice the process. Study the sample on the following page.

   Since these are descriptive paragraphs, try to be particularly mindful to include five-senses descriptions. Include what things look like, sound like, feel like, smell like, and taste like, where possible. Use page 155 for help. Also on page 155, learn a new sentence opener: #3 -ly adverb.

3. Paragraphs must follow the topic sentence-clincher rule. Keep in mind that you'll be adding a paragraph of introduction, so don't begin the first paragraph with an introductory sentence. Begin with a topic sentence.

   Similarly, you'll add a paragraph of conclusion, so no final clincher is needed yet.

Days 2–4

1. Polish the knight report from Lessons 19–20. Do not lose this. We will be adding an introduction and conclusion paragraph to the report in Lesson 25.

2. Complete the outline and paragraphs about your favorite forms of entertainment. Remember to ask yourself plenty of questions to get ideas about what to say. Also, try to include specific descriptions of what you say. Page 155 should help.

3. Follow the checklist on page 156.

4. You will use the two paragraphs in Lesson 23.

Study for Vocabulary Quiz 5. It covers words from Lessons 1–20.

Institute for Excellence in Writing

In Lesson 24, *Marco Polo* by Demi is suggested reading. It is a beautiful picture book. If your students did not purchase it, you can probably find it at the library and read some of it in class.

Lesson 22: Favorite Amusements, Part 1

Topic:

I. Disneyland, favorite, S. Tours

1. r. coaster, simulator, movie

What?
2. realistic, line, = boarding

Who?
3. ☺ wait, w/C3PO, R2D2+ ent. screens

Why?
4. screen + sound + vib

5. screen, w/space, buzzing

See?
6. = feels, real, w. speed

Hear?
7. hit, C3PO, takes

How feel?
8. safe, landing = ☺

Clincher

Here is a sample paragraph from the above outline. Note that some facts may be left out and more added. Facts may be written in a different order as well.

[Topic sentence] My favorite attraction at Disneyland is the Star Tours ride. It is an exciting indoor roller coaster, flight simulator, and movie all in one. The first thing I like about this ride is that is realistic. Even when waiting in line, I feel like I am truly waiting to board a "Star Ship." C3PO, R2D2, other robots, and many screens <u>transport</u> me into a Star Tours airport and keep me entertained. Once passengers board, we <u>dutifully</u> buckle up, and a giant screen with a movie makes us feel like we are taking off and zooming through space. The ship dives, turns, and vibrates with the action in the movie. [2] For example, when we need to escape danger, we hit warp speed, and the stars whiz by in a blur of <u>bright</u> white <u>while</u> we are pinned to the backs of our seats. Also, when the ship is "hit" by an asteroid, it shakes with a loud boom as C3PO cries out. Everyone screams and grips their seats as the ship seems to be diving out of control. But C3PO, <u>who</u> takes the controls, saves the day, and we return for a safe landing. Star Tours is awesomely realistic, entertaining, and fun.

Each student will write his own unique outline. For modeling purposes, here is a sample that completes the Disneyland idea. These will become the body paragraphs of the 4-paragraph composition that students will finish in Lesson 23.

Unit 7: Inventive Writing

Key Word Outline - Favorite Amusements

Who?	
What?	
When?	
Where?	
Why?	
How?	
How feel?	
See?	
Hear?	
Best thing?	
Worst thing?	

II. Topic A: _Disneyland, favorite, S. Tours_

  1. _coaster, simulator, movie_

  2. _realistic, line, = boarding_

  3. _☺ wait, w/C3PO, R2D2+ ent. screens_

  4. _screen + sound + vib_

  5. _screen, w/space, buzzing_

  6. _= feels, real, w. speed_

  7. _hit, C3PO, takes_

  8. _safe, landing = ☺_

Clincher A

III. Topic B: _clean, fun, atmosphere_

  1. _spotless, beautiful, grounds_

  2. _Disney, characters, enchant_

  3. _parades, fireworks_

  4. _ea, area, captivating, theme_

  5. _pirates, Indiana Jones, Tom Sawyer's Isle_

  6. _future, w/robots, rockets_

  7. _educational, displays, shows_

Clincher B

The #3 Sentence Opener

Before you write from your outline, learn a new sentence opener: the #3 -ly opener. A #3 sentence begins with an -ly adverb.

3   *Happily, we buckle up for the thrilling ride.*

An -ly adverb as the first word of a sentence cannot count as an -ly dress-up anymore. It will count as a #3 sentence opener. You will now, therefore, need to have two -ly adverbs in each paragraph you write: one at the beginning of a sentence (#3 -ly opener) and one in the middle of a sentence (dress-up).

The -ly opener should not be underlined like a dress-up; a 3 in the left margin is the indicator.

Practice

Write a #3 sentence below that might fit in your essay. Remember to put a 3 in the left margin across from it.

3   *Happily, we watch the fireworks.*

Stretch Your Ideas

Adding specific details and descriptions is the most difficult part of writing descriptive essays. To help with this, do the following:

Add specific details to one or more of the ideas in your outline to tell *why* or *how*. Include five-senses words, like we did when we described settings in Unit 3 stories. For example, instead of "Movies are fun," you could add specifics:

> *Movies take you to other worlds. The huge screens bring vivid pictures to life. Stirring music surrounds you. Movies can make you laugh, cry, fear a villain, cheer a hero, or hold your breath in suspense.*

Movies are fun by itself is vague. It is boring. It says little. The addition is much more specific. It tells *how* and *why* movies are fun. Try to add such details into a sentence in your paragraph. How or why is the entertainment you are writing about enjoyable? Be specific.

Unit 7: Inventive Writing

Lesson 22 Checklist (Body) - Favorite Amusements

FORMAT

☐ Modified MLA format (See Appendix 1.)   _____ (2 pts)

STRUCTURE

☐ ☐ Topic sentences with key words highlighted, each paragraph   _____ (6 pts)

☐ ☐ Clinchers with key words highlighted, each paragraph   _____ (6 pts)

STYLE Each paragraph must contain at least one of each element of style.

¶ 1   ¶ 2   Dress-Ups (Underline one of each; abbreviate in right margin.)   **(2 pts each)**

☐ ☐ -ly adverb   _____ (4 pts)

☐ ☐ *who–which* clause   _____ (4 pts)

☐ ☐ strong verb   _____ (4 pts)

☐ ☐ because clause   _____ (4 pts)

☐ ☐ quality adjective   _____ (4 pts)

☐ ☐ www.asia clause   _____ (4 pts)

Decorations (Include at least one per paragraph.) ("dec" in margin or italics)   **(2 pts each)**

☐ ☐ alliteration, simile, 3sss   _____ (4 pts)

Sentence Openers (numbered; one of each as possible)   **(2 pts each)**

☐ ☐ [2] prepositional   _____ (4 pts)

☐ ☐ [3] -ly adverb   _____ (4 pts)

MECHANICS

☐ banned words: go/went say/said nice/mean   _____ (-1 pt)

MORE ADVANCED ADDITIONS

☐ vocabulary words (*Label voc or bold.*)   _____

☐ dual adjective, verb, or -ly adverb   _____

☐ triple extension   _____

Total _____/50

Custom total _____ / _____

Lesson 23: Favorite Amusements, Part 2

Unit 7: Inventive Writing

Lesson 23: Favorite Amusements, Part 2

Review

1. Read your topic sentences and clinchers for Lesson 22 paragraphs. Tell the class which words you highlighted in each.

This is a good way to check that each student has clear topic sentences and clinchers for their body paragraphs. Discuss problems as necessary.

2. What are the question starter words that can help give you ideas for what to write about a subject or topic? Write them below.

   Who?   What?   When?   Where?   Why?   How?

   How feel?   Best thing?   Worst thing?

3. What other things will help you add detail to your paragraphs?

Adding specific examples and five-senses descriptions.

Introductions and Conclusions

In this lesson you will add a paragraph of introduction and a paragraph of conclusion to the paragraphs you wrote in Lesson 22. The job of an introduction is, of course, to introduce your paragraphs by telling what they are about. However, there is another important job an introduction must do. Because it is the first thing your readers will read, it must grab their attention and make them want to continue to read. For this reason you will begin the introduction for this assignment with a special kind of opening, an anecdote. Here is a sample introduction that includes such an opening for two paragraphs about Disneyland. Each component is labeled. They are discussed on the following page.

[**Anecdote**] I'll never forget my tenth birthday. It started out like any other day, but quickly turned magical. My mom and dad took me to the bagel shop for breakfast. When we walked in, there were my three best friends, all wearing huge smiles and silly homemade Mickey Mouse ears. "Happy Birthday!" they shouted, "We're going to Disneyland!" I turned to my parents to be sure it was true. They each gave me a nod and a smile. I ran to hug them. I was so excited that I could not sit still to eat. [**Subject and Background**] I love Disneyland. It is my favorite amusement park because it has the best rides and the most fun atmosphere. [**Topic A**] I always dash for Stars Tours first. I love feeling like I am on a real spaceship. [**Topic B**] However, wherever I am in the park, I feel like I am in a far-away, enchanted place.

Each student will write his own unique outline to match his essay. Walk around the room and check what they are writing. Help as necessary.

Unit 7: Inventive Writing

Introduction

The parts of a basic introduction include the following:

Something to grab your reader's attention: Begin your report with something intriguing that will make your reader want to read on. In this composition you will use an anecdote, which is a very short story like the one that began the sample introduction (see previous page, bottom).

Anecdotes make wonderful openers to compositions because almost everyone enjoys a good story. Good stories tug on our emotions and give vivid five-senses descriptions to draw us in. Begin your composition with a short story about a time when you particularly enjoyed the amusement you are writing about. Write in first person since it is a story about you.

Introduce the subject, and give background information: Make a statement about the subject of your composition. Then, give any background information you think would be helpful.

Mention the topics: The simplest way to meet this requirement is to list the topics, but a list is not very interesting reading. Try to write one complete sentence for each of your topics; that is, tell the main idea of each body paragraph. You might need to add phrases or sentences to connect these ideas smoothly.

Outline an introduction.

Use key word notes.

I.   Anecdotal opener: _____

_____

_____

Subject/Background _____

_____

Topic A: _____

Topic B: _____

Conclusion

You will end your composition with a paragraph of conclusion. Here are the components you must include:

Restate the topics: As in the introduction, you may write a sentence about each topic, or you may combine them into one sentence.

The most significant and why: What is the most important thing to remember about your subject and *why*?

Final clincher: End the report with a sentence or two that repeats or reflects some of the key words or ideas from the beginning of your introduction, which in this case is your anecdote.

Sample

[Topic A] At Disneyland, Star Tours takes me to other worlds and lets me feel like I'm flying. There is no better ride anywhere. **[Topic B]** In addition, every place in the park seems magical. **[Most important and why]** But Disneyland is not just about the rides and atmosphere. It is about having fun with friends and family. It is about escaping from everyday chores, celebrating special days, and creating memories. I will never forget that I celebrated my tenth birthday at the "happiest place on earth."

Outline a conclusion.

Use key word notes.

Topic A: _____

Topic B: _____

Most significant: _____

Why?:   _____

Final clincher *(Repeat or reflect ideas from the anecdotal opener.)*

The Assignment

Day 1

1. With a teacher's help, fill in the blank outline on page 158 for an introduction for your favorite amusement paragraphs from Lesson 22.

    a. Write brief notes for an idea for a short anecdote. Since it will likely be about you, you should write in first person (use "I").

Important: Lead a discussion in which students may share their ideas for this.

    b. Introduce the subject, and provide some background information.

    c. Mention each body topic at the end of the introduction.

2. On page 159, fill in the blank outline for a conclusion.

    a. Write a sentence for each topic.

    b. Next, write what you think is the most important thing about your favorite amusement and why.

    c. End with a final clincher that reflects the idea of your anecdotal opener.

Days 2–4

1. Polish the research report from Lesson 21: King Richard and King John.

2. Add your introduction and conclusion to the beginning and end of the two paragraphs from Lesson 22. In other words, put all paragraphs together into one composition.

3. There are no new vocabulary words for Lesson 23. Continue to review all.

Each student will write his own unique outline to match his composition. Walk around the room, and check what they are writing. Help as necessary.

Teacher Note:

Next week, *Marco Polo* by Demi is suggested reading. It is a beautiful picture book. If your students did not purchase it, you can probably find it at the library and read some of it in class next week.

Lesson 23 Final Checklist -
Favorite Amusements with Introduction and Conclusion

FORMAT

☐ Modified MLA format (See Appendix 1.) _____ (2 pts)

STRUCTURE

☐ Title repeats or reflects key words from final clincher (or dramatic close). _____ (3 pts)

   I.   Introduction

☐ Anecdotal opener _____ (10 pts)

☐ Subject and background info _____ (5 pts)

☐ Topics mentioned (Label A, B.) _____ (6 pts)

☐ Any four dress-ups, one dec., and two openers _____ (6 pts)

      Body

☐ Checklist from Lesson 22 (p. 156) is attached. _____ (3 pts)
    (This will be used to grade the body paragraphs.)

   IV. Conclusion

☐ Restate topics. (Label A, B.) _____ (6 pts)

☐ Any four dress-ups, one dec., and two openers _____ (6 pts)

☐ Most significant and why _____ (5 pts)

☐ Final clincher (Reflect the beginning of the introduction.) _____ (3 pts)

MECHANICS

☐ banned words: go/went say/said nice/mean _____ (-1 pt)

MORE ADVANCED ADDITIONS

☐ vocabulary words (*Label voc or bold.*) _____

☐ dual adjective, verb, or -ly adverb _____

☐ triple extension _____

Total _____ /55

Custom total _____ / _____

Unit 7: Inventive Writing

Unit 7: Inventive Writing

Lesson 24: The Twenty-First-Century Descriptive Letter

Lesson 24: The Twenty-First-Century Descriptive Letter

Review

Play the five-senses game described in the TM.

Teachers, see page 278. Use the following categories and words, or similar:

food/drink: popcorn, Coke, pizza, hot dog

objects outside: skyscraper, bus, train, helicopter, lawn mower

inside: refrigerator, lamp, canned food

In this lesson you will write a letter from your own thoughts and ideas. Here is the prompt.

Prompt

Marco Polo traveled far from his home in Italy to Asia. When he reached the empire of Kublai Khan (grandson of Genghis Khan), he could not believe what he was seeing and experiencing. He was in awe of the strange new land. Later, he wrote a book describing his experiences, but most of the people in Europe at that time did not believe his splendid descriptions.

Pretend you are a peasant of the Middle Ages who has traveled into the twenty-first century. After being there for a week, write a letter to your family telling them about the things you have seen and experienced. Do not use terms that medieval people would not be familiar with.

If you did not have students purchase *Marco Polo* by Demi, read some of this book in class. Notice how *Marco Polo* describes things he is unfamiliar with.

Unit 7: Inventive Writing

The Assignment

Day 1

1. After reading the prompt, note that the blank outline on page 166 has provided a brief introduction and two topics for your letter:

    A. the first day

    B. the remainder of the week

2. Even though there is no source text from which to take notes, you must organize your ideas into an outline. Using the questions on page 165 to help you, fill in ideas on the blank outline on page 166.

3. Before you write your letter, practice using a new sentence opener, the #4 -ing sentence opener on page 167.

Days 2–4

1. Optional: Read *Marco Polo* by Demi. (See Appendix 4 for a description.)

2. Use your outline and your brainstorming ideas to guide you in writing your descriptive letter.

3. Follow the checklist on page 168. Attach it to your final draft.

4. There are no new vocabulary words for Lesson 24.

Advanced lesson for experienced students: See the *Medieval History-Based Advanced Lessons Blackline Masters* to practice more advanced elements of style.

Important: Bring your knights report from Lessons 19–20 to class next week.

Literature Suggestion

With Lessons 24–27 read *The Kite Rider* by Geraldine McCaughrean.

These are simply sample questions to help students get ideas. They do not have to answer all of them, and they may think of other things to discuss. Read the sample essay from Appendix 3 on page 240.

For ideas about what to say in your letter, use the questions below and others like them. Note your ideas on the blank outline on the following page. The paragraphs are about I. the first day and II. the rest of the week.

Questions

I.

1. Where did you arrive?

2. When did you arrive—day or night?

3. What did you see and hear? Describe with five-senses words.

4. Who did you meet?

5. How did the people react?

6. Did anyone befriend you, or did people make fun of you? Did they believe you?

7. What did they tell you?

8. Where did you go? Did you go alone or with someone?

9. What did you think about everything you saw?

10. How did you feel? How did your feeling show?

II.

1. What did you do each day?

2. What did you learn?

3. What did you like or not like about life in the twenty-first century?

4. What impressed you most? Why?

5. What confused you most? Why?

6. How do you plan to return to medieval times—or do you?

    (Questions 5–10 under Section I could also be discussed in this paragraph.)

Unit 7: Inventive Writing

Key Word Outline - The Twenty-First-Century Descriptive Letter

Dear _____ ,

I am in the twenty-first century! I got here by

Who?
What?
When?
Where?
Why?
How?
How feel?
See?
Hear?
Best thing?
Worst thing?

I. Topic A: _1st, day, massive, city_

   1. _towering, bldgs, ppl, everywhere_

   2. _⊘ fields, forests_

   3. _carriages, w/wheels, ⊘ horses_

   4. _noisy, honk, geese_

   5. _met, boy, 12, Luke_

   6. _said, Merlin, sent_

   7. _→ home, explained, cars_

Clincher A

II. Topic B: _rest, week, Luke_

   1. _breakfast, eggs, ⊘, hens!_

   2. _metal, box, cold_

   3. _called, refrigerator, 4 food_

   4. _Lk, ⊘, plow, sow_

   5. _play, day, w/box_

   6. _lights, pictures, games_

   7. _computer, my, favorite_

Clincher B

Final clincher *(Reflect twenty-first century.)*

The #4 Sentence Opener

Before you write from your outline, learn a new sentence opener: the #4 *-ing opener*.
A #4 sentence is a sentence that begins with an -ing phrase.

The -ing word must be an action word.

The -ing phrase must be followed by a comma, and it must be in front of a complete sentence.

The subject of that sentence must be doing the -ing phrase.

Notice how all of these things are true about the sentences below.

4   *Hoping to find help in this strange new world, I plodded on.*

4   *Seeing a roaring metal bird over me, I scrambled for cover.*

Imposter #4s

The #4 sentence can be tricky. There are some imposters, such as prepositions that end in -ing (*during, concerning, regarding*). The following sentence is actually a #2 opener:

During the fantastic trip, I learned about a completely different way of life.

Some adjectives end in -ing:

Honking metal carriages surrounded me.

The above sentence is not a #4 sentence. It does not have an -ing phrase followed by a comma followed by a complete sentence. *Honking* is simply describing the carriages.

Sometimes an -ing word is the subject of a sentence:

Running is a sport here.

Again, there is no phrase followed by a comma followed by a complete sentence, so it is not a #4 opener.

Practice

Write an idea for a #4 sentence you could use in your composition. Remember to put a *4* in the left margin across from it.

4   *Wearing a huge smile, my best friend was waiting for me in the restaurant.*

Lesson 24 Final Checklist -
The Twenty-First-Century Descriptive Letter

FORMAT

- [ ] Modified MLA format (See Appendix 1.)   _____ (2 pts)

STRUCTURE

- [ ] Title repeats or reflects key words from final clincher.   _____ (3 pts)
- [ ] Topic sentences with key words highlighted, each paragraph   _____ (6 pts)
- [ ] Clinchers with key words highlighted, each paragraph   _____ (4 pts)
- [ ] Final clincher reflects introductory sentence.   _____ (5 pts)

STYLE Each paragraph must contain at least one of each element of style.

¶ 1 ¶ 2 Dress-Ups (Underline one of each; abbreviate in right margin.)   **(2 pts each)**

- [ ] [ ] -ly adverb   _____ (4 pts)
- [ ] [ ] *who–which* clause   _____ (4 pts)
- [ ] [ ] strong verb   _____ (4 pts)
- [ ] [ ] because clause   _____ (4 pts)
- [ ] [ ] quality adjective   _____ (4 pts)
- [ ] [ ] www.asia clause   _____ (4 pts)

Decorations (Use at least one per para.) ("dec" in margin or italics)   **(2 pts each)**

- [ ] [ ] alliteration, simile, or 3sss   _____ (4 pts)

Sentence Openers (numbered; one of each as possible)   **(2 pts each)**

- [ ] [ ] [2] prepositional   _____ (4 pts)
- [ ] [ ] [3] -ly adverb   _____ (4 pts)
- [ ] [ ] [4] -ing ,   _____ (4 pts)

MECHANICS

- [ ] banned words: go/went say/said nice/mean   _____ (-1 pt)

MORE ADVANCED ADDITIONS

- [ ] vocabulary words (*Label voc or bold.*)   _____
- [ ] dual adjective, verb, or -ly adverb   _____
- [ ] triple extension   _____

Total _____/60

Custom total _____ / _____

Teachers, review Unit 8: Formal Essays in the TWSS workbook. If you have the seminar on DVD, watch the corresponding lesson.

You should be returning the knights body paragraphs written in Lessons 19–20 and polished with Lesson 22. In this lesson, students will add a paragraph of introduction and a paragraph of conclusion to them. (If you omitted Lesson 21, students just polished the body, so you will have to check the polishing when they turn in the entire 5-paragraph report from this lesson.)

Have some students read their Twenty-First-Century essays before collecting them.

Unit 8: Formal Essays

Lesson 25: Knights, Part 3

Review

Play hangman from the TM.

Use the following phrase: SENTENCE OPENERS

Once solved, ask which sentence openers they have learned thus far and how they should be labeled. (prepositional- 2 in margin; -ly adverb- 3 in margin; -ing opener- 4 in margin; no underlines)

Basic Essay Model

The basic essay model consists of five paragraphs: three body paragraphs plus an introduction and conclusion. However, the model can be adapted by simply changing the number of body paragraphs. Each body paragraph must have its own distinct topic, but not every subject divides neatly into three topics.

Today you will add an introduction and conclusion to the three body paragraphs you wrote in Lessons 19 and 20 about knights.

The job of the introduction is basically to introduce the topics. The job of the conclusion is basically to remind the reader of the topics and then to clarify the most important thing about the subject and why.

But the introduction has another equally important purpose. An introduction must grab the reader's attention; it must entice him to keep reading. If you begin with something boring, it is likely that your reader will put down the essay without finishing it. In Lesson 23, you learned to add an anecdote as an opening. In this lesson you will learn a different type of opening.

Study the following two pages to understand the elements of introduction and conclusion paragraphs.

As you read each element, point it out in the sample introduction or conclusion paragraph on the following page.

Unit 8: Formal Essays

Introduction

Grab your reader's attention: Begin your report with something intriguing that will make your reader want to read on. To help with this, we will learn a new decoration. It is one type of dramatic opener called a very short sentence.

Introduce the subject, and give background information: Tell your reader the subject of the report, but do not say anything similar to "*this report is about*." Simply make a general statement about the subject. Then, give any background information you think would be helpful. For ideas, look at how each of the source texts on pages 128–132 begins.

Mention the topics: The simplest way to meet this requirement is to list the topics, but a list is not very interesting reading. Try to write one complete sentence for each of your topics; tell the main idea of each body paragraph. You may need to add phrases or sentences to connect these ideas smoothly.

Conclusion

Restate the topics: As in the introduction, the best way to do this is to write a sentence about each topic.

The most significant and why: What is the most important thing to remember about your subject and *why*? For the knights report, think about why knights are still remembered and studied today. What can we learn from their legacy?

Final clincher: End the report with a sentence that repeats or reflects two to three key words from the beginning of your introduction. You may also add a dramatic closer to reflect a dramatic opener.

Sample Introduction and Conclusion

Notice each of the required elements. The subject of the report is the Black Death. The bold words are the words in the beginning that are reflected in the final clincher—the subject of the report. (A dramatic opener and closer are added before and after each.)

Introduction

Dramatic open	*Everyone feared it*. But it was not a mighty, fierce **army** of knights;
Subject	rather, it was a **sickness**. It was called the "Black Death" because those
Background	who caught it became covered with black lumps and were sure to die.
Topic A	Today, we know it was the bubonic plague, a highly contagious disease.
Topic B	From 1347–1350 it spread through Europe, carried by rats brought from
Topic C	Asia by Italian merchants. This horrible plague killed at least one-third
	of the entire population of Europe.

The Body The topics of the body paragraphs are as follows:

A. What the Black Death Was

B. When and How the Black Death Spread

C. The Effect of the Black Death

Conclusion

Topic A	"The Black Death" (the bubonic plague) was the most catastrophic
Topic B	event of the Middle Ages. Because it was so contagious and people did not
	know what caused it, it spread like wildfire through Europe. With
Topic C	more than a third of the people of Europe dead, the plague had long-
Most signif.	lasting effects. Most significantly, with so few people left, peasants had
	opportunities to become craftsmen, and the feudal system began to erode.
Why?	The plague, therefore, helped bring in a new era of hope for many. But
Clincher	while some of the long-term effects may have been positive, when the
	plague was present, it struck fear into every heart, as it killed more people
Dramatic close	than all the **armies** of the Middle Ages put together. *It was terrifying*.

Unit 8: Formal Essays

The Assignment

Day 1

1. With a teacher, fill in the blank outlines on page 174 for an introduction to your knight report:

   a. Begin with something that will grab your readers' attention. Use page 173 to help give you an idea for this.

   b. To introduce the subject and background, give any general information about knights that would help lead into your topics. Consider how each source text on pages 128–132 begins.

   c. Mention each of your body topics.

2. With a teacher, fill out the blank outline for a conclusion.

   a. Restate each topic. You may write a sentence for each, or combine all into one sentence.

   b. Next, write what you think is the most important thing about knights and why. Why do we still study knights today? What can we learn from them?

   c. End with a final clincher that reflects the idea in the beginning of your introduction (the subject of your report).

   d. Add a dramatic closer if you used a dramatic opening (very short sentence).

3. Read your notes as complete sentences to be sure you understand how to use your outlines to write an introduction and conclusion. Study the samples on page 171.

Days 2–4

1. Polish your favorite amusements composition from Lessons 22–23.

2. Add your introduction and conclusion to the beginning and end of the paragraphs you wrote about knights in Lessons 19 and 20. In other words, put all five paragraphs together into one essay. Follow the checklist on page 175.

   Note that you may use the final clincher or dramatic closer (if you added one) in order to create a title.

3. There are no new vocabulary words for Lesson 25.

Dramatic Open-Close: Very Short Sentence (VSS)

An introduction should begin by grabbing your reader's attention. It may be difficult to think of a sentence that will do this. If that is the case, you may try a decoration called a *dramatic open*.

The dramatic open is designed to grab a reader's attention. *Everyone feared it.* Did it grab your attention? Why or why not?

This is the easiest dramatic open: a *very short sentence* (vss). This is a sentence with 2–5 words. Short sentences stand out. They draw attention to themselves.

When you use a dramatic open, you might have to add a sentence or two between the dramatic short sentence and the sentence that introduces the subject in order to make the sentences flow smoothly. Be sure your paragraph flows well.

If you begin with a dramatic vss, you might want to end the entire report with another short sentence that reflects it. This is called a *dramatic close*. The dramatic open-close go together to frame the report.

Write two different dramatic very short sentences that could open and close your report about knights. If you like one, use it!

Open:	*Knights are legendary.*	*Close:*	*Their legend lives on.*
	"I dub thee, knight."		*Knighthood was a special calling.*
	Knights served the king.		*Knights were loyal servants.*
	They risked their lives.		*Knights were noble.*
	Knights were fearless fighters.		*We still admire their bravery.*

Outline for Introduction

Grab attention: *M-A, **rememb**, >, **knights**, shining, armor*
                       (Note: This in not a vss dramatic opener. That decoration is optional. See below.)

Subject/Background: *elite, soldiers, horseback*

                       A.D. 900–1500s

Topic A: *job, protect, land*

Topic B: *trained, from, boyhood*

Topic C: *followed, Code, Chivalry*
                       (Note: This is merely a sample. Students will write their own ideas and introduce the topics they wrote about.)

Outline for Conclusion

Topic A: *kept, kingdom, safe*

Topic B: *well-trained*

Topic C: *Code =valiant, noble*

Most significant: *served others; helped helpless*

Why?   *Role models, 2day*

Final clincher

Dramatic close (*if you tried the dramatic open to grab attention*)

    Institute for Excellence in Writing

With the option of a dramatic open to fulfill "Grab attention," the first line could be one of the sample ideas students had from page 173. In that case, a dramatic close would be added to the end of the conclusion. Please see page 173 samples for ideas. Students are welcome to use one of the samples provided.

Lesson 25 Final Checklist -
Knights

FORMAT

☐ Modified MLA format (See Appendix 1.) _____ (2 pts)

STRUCTURE

☐ Title repeats or reflects key words from final clincher (or dramatic close). _____ (3 pts)

I. Introduction

☐ Grab attention _____ (3 pts)

☐ Subject and background info _____ (5 pts)

☐ Topics mentioned *(Label A, B, C)* _____ (6 pts)

☐ Any four dress-ups, one dec., and two openers _____ (6 pts)

II.–IV. Body

☐ (from Lessons 19–20) _____ (5 pts)

The body paragraphs should have been polished. Now they should be inserted between the introduction and conclusion.

V. Conclusion

☐ Restate topics. *(Label A, B, C)* _____ (6 pts)

☐ Any four dress-ups, one dec., and two openers _____ (6 pts)

☐ Most significant and why _____ (5 pts)

☐ Final clincher reflects the beginning of the introduction. _____ (3 pts)

(If you used a dramatic open, add a dramatic close.)

MECHANICS

☐ banned words: go/went say/said nice/mean _____ (-1 pt)

MORE ADVANCED ADDITIONS

☐ vocabulary words *(Label voc or bold.)* _____

☐ dual adjective, verb, or -ly adverb _____

☐ triple extension _____

Total _____/50

Custom total _____ / _____

Unit 8: Formal Essays

Teachers, review Unit 9: Formal Critiques in the TWSS workbook before teaching Lesson 26. If you have the seminar on DVD, watch the corresponding lesson.

If you have a young class, spend two weeks on this lesson. Do I–IV this week and V the following.

Unit 9: Formal Critiques

Lesson 26: "Genghis Khan and His Hawk"

Review
Play a vocabulary game from the TM.

The Critique Model
This lesson begins a new unit, one in which you will be combining the skills of three previous units. You have learned the elements of a well-written story: the Story Sequence Chart. You have learned to write reports by reading and taking notes from sources and structuring the notes into paragraphs with clear topics. And you have learned to take notes and write from your own thoughts and ideas. In this unit, you are going to learn to use all three of these skills to help you write critiques of literature.

When you critique a story, you do not retell it; instead, you give your opinion about it. You tell what you like or do not like about it. Before you do so, though, you explain only the most important aspects of the Story Sequence Chart—just enough so your reader can follow your discussion of your opinion about the story. This is the body of the critique, and it is like a "report" about the story.

A critique follows the basic essay model with an introduction, three body paragraphs, and a conclusion. Each body paragraph has a predetermined topic, and the elements required in the introduction and conclusion are specific to critiques.

Here is a model of the structure:

  I.   Introduction (title, author, publisher, background)

  II. Characters/Setting

  III. Conflict/Plot

  IV. Climax/Resolution

This middle section is a brief summary of the Story Sequence Chart from Unit 3.

  V.   Conclusion (your opinion)

This model can be used to critique any type of story: short stories, movies, novels, plays, TV shows, or anything that tells a story.

The most difficult, but most important, part of a critique is the conclusion. Here you should tell what you like or dislike about the story, but do not say anything like, "I think" or "in my opinion." For example, if you say, "It was a suspenseful story with plenty of action and a clever riddle to ponder," your readers will know your opinion, but it will sound much more convincing than, "I think it was a good story."

On the next page is a sample critique. Can you tell whether the author liked the story? How?

"outlandishly humorous"; "funny"; "hilarious amusement"; "cleverly crafted"; "stylishly entertaining"

Note also that the body paragraphs have clear topic sentences for characters or setting, conflict, and climax. Each element of the Story Sequence Chart is discussed.

Source Text

A Stylish Swine Story

A *Triune Tale of Diminutive Swine* is John Branyan's version of the classic children's story, "The Three Little Pigs," told in Old English. The book was published by Rockshow Comedy, Inc. in 2012.

The characters of this tale are the three pigs and a wolf. Two of the pigs are rather foolish and lazy when it comes to building their homes. However, the third pig is wise and diligent. The evil wolf is strong and determined. The story is set "in a time not long past when there lived pigs in stature little and number three who of an age now both entitled and inspired to seek their fortunes did set out to do so ... thusly."

The conflict is that the wolf desires to eat the pigs, who have just set out to live on their own. Because the first two pigs gave no thought and little effort to building their homes, the wolf easily blows them down. Fortunately, these porkers are able to run to the shelter of their brother's brick home, which is a strong fortress.

The climax occurs when the wolf tries to blow down the third house but is stymied by the strong walls. The pigs are safe, and the first two learn the value of hard work and foresight. This is clearly the theme of the tale. But behind the tale is also a theme of language.

A *Triune Tale of Diminutive Swine* is an outlandishly humorous retelling of a familiar story. It is funny because it is told in Old English. For example, the classic line, "Not by the hair of my chinny chin chin" becomes, "Nay, it shall not be! Not by whit nor whiskered jowl!" and, "Then he huffed and he puffed and he blew the house down" becomes, "Whereupon the wolf did billow forth an exhale of gale force which quickly rendered straw hovel to dregs and dross, and carried aloft piglet and shattered quarters both." Such flowery language does make parts difficult to understand, so young readers may become lost and frustrated. However, since the story is so familiar, the effect of the style on more mature readers is hilarious amusement, especially for those who enjoy language. Like all versions of "The Three Little Pigs," this one teaches the value of hard work, but it also pokes fun at language. In addition, it has a surprise humorous twist to the end. Branyan's silly story of swine is stylishly entertaining.

The Assignment

Note: This more lengthy assignment is broken into two parts so that younger students may spend two weeks on it. They should outline and write paragraphs I–IV the first week. These paragraphs should be fairly short. They should complete the conclusion, which will be longer, the second week.

Day 1

1. Read the story, "Genghis Khan and His Hawk" on page 180.

2. Using the blank outline on page 181 as a guide, write a key word outline for the first four paragraphs of your critique. These paragraphs will be short.

Be sure to write notes in present tense, and teach students that when writing about events in stories, they must use present tense. See Step #2 below.

3. Using pages 182–183, outline the conclusion of the critique. Discuss each question on page 182 in order to get ideas for what to say. This should be your longest paragraph. (Younger students should do this the week after completing I–IV.)

4. Look at the vocabulary words for Lesson 26: *analyze, aghast, tragic, rash*. How could you use these in your critique?

Be sure to go over the homework below, and be sure everyone understands the checklist on page 184.

Days 2–4

1. Polish the entire knights report from Lesson 25.

2. Use your outlines to write a critique. (Younger students may need to spend two weeks on this.) When writing about events in the story, use present tense:

    *The story **is** (not was) a moral story with a valuable lesson.*

    *The hawk **knocks** (not knocked) the cup from his master's hand.*

3. Follow the checklist on page 184 carefully.

    Notice that because the first paragraphs are short, you are only required to use one of each element of style anywhere within all four paragraphs rather than one of each in every paragraph. However, since the conclusion should be longer, you need one of each element of style in the conclusion.

4. Cut out and learn the vocabulary words for Lesson 26.

Advanced lesson: Use the *Medieval History-Based Advanced Lessons Blackline Masters* to practice avoiding "you." In addition, use the SRN to include some critique vocabulary.

Study for the final vocabulary test.

Source Text

Genghis Khan and His Hawk
retold by Lori Verstegen

Genghis Khan ruled the huge Mongolian empire in the early 1200s. He was a ruthless warrior and a respected king who commanded multitudes. When he was not at war, the khan enjoyed his favorite sport of hunting. And when he hunted, his loyal hawk always accompanied him. His hawk was his best friend. He loved his master, and he loved hunting. With his keen eyes and his master's great skill, their hunting expeditions were always a success.

One day while on a hunt, the khan wandered farther than he had intended. In an intense chase, a deer had led him out of the shade of the forest trees, and he found himself in a barren field with the sun beating down on his head. He was hot and thirsty. He had to find water soon, so he stopped pursuing the deer, which had disappeared anyway, and headed back to the forest to look for a stream.

As he approached the forest, he heard the soft, constant trickling of water. He followed the sound. It led him to a high cluster of massive rocks, over which a small flow of crystal clear water fell. It was a welcome sight! The khan quickly took his cup from his pack and placed it under the stream. When the cup was filled, he brought it to his lips, anticipating how cool and refreshing it would be. However, before he could take a drink, his hawk swooped down and knocked the cup from his hand. The khan was stunned and angered by this apparently cruel action and shouted, "You crazy bird! You've spilled my water all over the ground!"

So the khan picked up his cup again, and again filled it with the water. But again, when he lifted it to his lips, his hawk flew down and knocked the cup from his hand.

"Insolent bird!" he yelled as he waved his arms at his hawk. "You'll not deprive me of a drink a third time." And with that the khan readied his sword. When the bird dove for the cup a third time, the khan struck him with his sword. The bird plummeted to the ground, dead.

Now by the time the khan retrieved his cup, the flow of water had diminished so much that the cup was only filling one drop at a time. Impatiently, the khan decided to climb up higher to find the source of the flow. As he neared the top ledge, he spotted a large pool. As he looked closer, he was aghast at what he saw. In the pool was a dead viper, cut at the throat so that all of its deadly venom had spilled into the water.

"What have I done?" he lamented, for at that moment he realized that his hawk had only been trying to save his life. "I have killed my best friend. What a rash fool I was not to have trusted him and to have let my temper consume me so."

With that, he climbed down the rocks, picked up the stricken bird, and headed home. He had lost a friend, but he had learned a valuable lesson he would never forget.

Note that titles of short stories should be in quotation marks.

Introduction

Background may be any information about the story that would be of interest, such as who Genghis Khan actually was, or it could be what happens in the story before the conflict actually begins. Also, be sure kids understand that they do not have to write the notes in order when they write the paragraph. For example, they could write: "Genghis Khan and His Hawk" is a classic moral tale. The original author is unknown.

Lesson 26: "Genghis Khan and His Hawk"

Critique Outline

Title, Author, Publisher, Date
Type of story
Background

I. _"GK & Hawk," author ?, retold, L.V._
   1. _pub, IEW, 2015_
   2. _classic, moral, tale_

Topic (the characters and setting)
Who is in the story?
What are they like?
When does it happen?
Where do they live or go?

II. _GK, hawk, Mongolia, hunt_
   1. _GK, ruler, ruthless, warrior, 1200s_
   2. _⊘ control, temper_
   3. _hawk, loyal, companion_
   4. _loves, hunt, w/GK_

Topic (the problem or want)
What causes the problem or want?
What do the characters do, say, think,
   and feel before the climax?

III. _GK, needs, water_
   1. _hunting, strays, thirsty_
   2. _finds, fills, cup_
   3. _hawk, knocks, 2x_
   4. _khan, irate, sword_
   5. _3rd, khan, XX, hawk_

Climax

The climax would be the point at which we know how the conflict will work out. It may seem like killing his hawk is the climax, but when the khan does this, it looks like he will get the water. We do not realize that he won't until he climbs to the source and sees the viper.

Topic
(What leads to the conflict working out as it did?)
What happens next?
What is the end result?
What is the main theme or message?

IV. _GK, viper, slit_
   1. _⊙ ⊙, viper, slit_
   2. _poisoning, water_
   3. _realizes, hawk, saved, ☹_
   4. _act, anger ➔ regret_

Remind students.

Do not use *I* or *my* with this.

Lesson 26b: The Conclusion

In the conclusion, discuss what you like or dislike about the story and why. It should be your longest paragraph. It is the most difficult part because it requires you to analyze. The following questions should help you fill in the outline on page 183.

V. What did you think of the story? Begin your conclusion with a general statement that reveals your overall opinion of the story. Do not use vague adjectives like *good*, *interesting*, *wonderful*, and the like. Do not say *I*, *my*, or *you*. (Note the beginnings of the sample conclusions on page 178 and page 244 of Appendix 3. For help, see the SRN page about "Critique Vocabulary."

Support your opinion by discussing some of the following:

Characters and Setting

What makes the characters interesting?

What about the setting is worthy of mention?

Khan is a real historical figure. He can control an empire, but not himself. The setting reveals a little about the culture of the 1200s. Most people can relate to having a pet. We all lose our temper at times.

What makes each character likeable or unlikeable? Is that important to the point of the story? Why?

Hawk is kind and loyal. If the hawk was simply a wild animal, readers would not care when he is killed. The khan cannot control his temper and kills the hawk.

Conflict/Plot

What makes the conflict and plot intriguing?   *surprise ending*

Why didn't the author reveal to the reader that the water was poisoned when the khan first found the trickle? What did keeping it hidden add to the story?   *intrigue*

Climax and Resolution

How could you describe the climax, i.e., surprising, exciting, predictable, dull? What emotions will readers feel at the climax? Why?

Let students give their own opinions and emotions.

Theme or Message

Is it clearly or powerfully communicated? How?   *tragic death of loyal pet*

Is there another lesson or truth communicated?   *loyalty*

End with your overall impression, a final clincher. (Reflect the topic sentence of this paragraph.)

Conclusion

What do you think of the story?

Things you like or dislike

Why? Examples from story

Discuss the message or theme(s).

Final clincher reflects your opinion.

V. Topic: *"GK & H," tragic, w/imp, message, ⊘ forgotten*

1. *char, intriguing, b/c, GK, real*

2. *GK, rule, emp. ⊘ control, self*

3. *hawk, likeable, knocks*

4. *emotional ☹, when, XX*

5. *surprising, finds, viper*

6. *theme, obvious, convicting*

7. *all, ⊘, act, anger*

8. *+ trust, friends*

Remember:

Do not say *I* or *my*.

Write in *present* tense.

Example: Instead of saying "*I think it is a _____ story,*" state your opinion

as a fact: "*It is a _____ story.*"

Lesson 26 Final Checklist -
"Genghis Khan and His Hawk" Critique

STRUCTURE

☐	Title repeats or reflects key words from final clincher.	_____ (5 pts)
☐ I.	**Introduction**: title, author, publisher, background	_____ (5 pts)
☐ II.	**Characters, Settings**	_____ (5 pts)
☐ III.	**Conflict, Plot**	_____ (5 pts)
☐ IV.	**Climax, Resolution, Theme or Message**	_____ (5 pts)
☐ V.	**Conclusion**: Begin with your overall opinion.	_____ (5 pts)
☐	Discuss at least three elements you like or do not like.	_____ (5 pts)
☐	Include examples from the story.	_____ (5 pts)
☐	Final clincher reflects your opinion.	_____ (5 pts)

Explain the two columns for elements of style. Students must use and label one of each anywhere within the first four paragraphs plus one of each in the last paragraph, since this paragraph will be the longest and most developed.

STYLE Each paragraph must contain at least one of each element of style.

¶I–IV. V.   Dress-Ups (Underline one of each; abbreviate in right margin.)   (2 pts each)

☐ ☐	-ly adverb		_____ (4 pts)
☐ ☐	*who–which* clause		_____ (4 pts)
☐ ☐	strong verb		_____ (4 pts)
☐ ☐	because clause		_____ (4 pts)
☐ ☐	quality adjective		_____ (4 pts)
☐ ☐	www.asia clause		_____ (4 pts)

Decorations (Use at least one per para.) ("dec" in margin or italics)   (2 pts each)

☐ ☐	alliteration, simile, or 3sss	_____ (4 pts)

Sentence Openers (numbered; one of each as possible)   (2 pts each)

☐ ☐	[2] prepositional	_____ (4 pts)
☐ ☐	[3] -ly adverb	_____ (4 pts)
☐ ☐	[4] -ing ,	_____ (4 pts)

MECHANICS

☐	banned words: I, my, you, your	_____ (-1 pt)
☐	banned words: go/went say/said nice/mean	_____ (-1 pt)

MORE ADVANCED ADDITIONS

☐	vocabulary words (*Label voc or bold.*)	_____
☐	dual adjective, verb, or -ly adverb	_____
☐	triple extension	_____

Total _____ /85

Custom total _____ / _____

Unit 9: Response to Literature

Lesson 27: "The Determined Samurai" (Theme Analysis)

Take the final vocabulary test.

Modifying the Critique Model: Theme Analysis

In Lesson 26 you learned to write a basic critique. In this lesson, you will use and modify this model in order to focus on analyzing the theme of a story.

What is a theme? A theme is what a story teaches. It is usually a universal truth (a truth that can be applied to people anytime and anywhere). Themes usually focus on virtues to be admired or evil to be shunned. Some examples of common themes of virtue are courage, loyalty, forgiveness, the power of love, the brotherhood of man, growing up, self-control, and the like. Some common themes of evil are prejudice, corruption, greed, dishonesty, revenge, abuse of power, and the like.

Because themes have the power to persuade readers, it is important to learn to analyze themes and to try to determine what an author is teaching through his story.

In this lesson, you will write a composition that is similar to a critique: a response to literature composition. The model you will follow is modified to allow for a paragraph to discuss the theme of the story. Here is the model you will follow:

I.   Introduction (title, author, publisher, background)

II. Characters/Setting, Conflict/Plot, Climax/Resolution

III. Theme Analysis

   Concluding statement (final clincher)

Notice that in the above model you will summarize the story in one paragraph rather than in three as before. This means that you will have to discuss only the most important elements, and do so very briefly. You will have to leave much out. You will not retell all the details of the story.

The following page is a sample response to "Genghis Khan and His Hawk" following the above model.

Literature Suggestion

You might like to plan ahead. With Lessons 28–31, *Crispin: the Cross of Lead* will be suggested as added literature.

Unit 9: Response to Literature

Sample

A Valuable Lesson

"Genghis Khan and His Hawk," which is retold by Lori Verstegen, was published by the Institute for Excellence in Writing in 2007. It is a moral story based on a legend. Genghis Khan is the ruler of a vast empire. In the story, he is enjoying a hunting trip with his hawk when he makes a tragic mistake and learns a valuable lesson.

Obviously the two dominant characters are the khan and his hawk. Genghis Khan, who is a powerful ruler in Mongolia in the 1200s, is short-tempered and rash. On the other hand, his hawk is loving, loyal, and persistent. He always does what is best for his master. The conflict is that the khan desperately needs water. When he finally finds some trickling down some rocks, his hawk knocks his cup from his hand every time he tries to drink. The khan becomes perturbed and kills him with his sword. The climax happens when he reaches the source of the stream and discovers that a dead viper has poisoned the water. He then realizes that his hawk had only been trying to save his life. Because he has acted out of anger, he has killed his best friend.

The khan learns the hard way that acting rashly in anger often leads to tragedy. This is the main theme. He learns this the moment he realizes that his temper has caused him to kill his best friend, who had been trying to protect him. The lesson is something that everyone should remember because anger can cause even the kindest people to do things they regret. In this story, the death of the hawk, who is a loving, loyal friend to the khan, is a very emotional event and, therefore, makes the theme memorable. The theme would not have been so powerful if the hawk had only been injured. So, even though it is sad that the hawk dies, his death is what makes the message so impactful. There is another theme as well: loyal friends should be trusted. Had the khan trusted his hawk, both would have been saved. Loyal friends are priceless possessions. Unfortunately, the khan has lost his most loyal friend. "Genghis Khan and His Hawk" is a tragic story with a valuable lesson.

Lesson 27: "The Determined Samurai" (Theme Analysis)

The Assignment

Day 1

1. Read the story, "The Determined Samurai" on the following page.

2. Using the blank outline on page 189 as a guide, write a key word outline together.

Be sure to write notes in present tense and teach students that when writing about events in stories, they must use present tense. See Step #2 below.

3. On page 190, learn the #5 sentence opener, and brainstorm ideas for a #5 sentence you could use in your composition.

Be sure to go over the homework below as well as the checklist. Note that each element of style is only required once anywhere throughout the essay, not in every paragraph. However, you could challenge students who are able to include each in every paragraph.

Days 2–4

1. If you haven't done so already, polish the entire knights essay from Lesson 25.

2. Use your outlines to write a response to literature composition. When writing about events in the story, use present tense:

   The story is (not was) a fun story with a thought-provoking lesson.

   The samurai laments (not lamented) his loss.

3. Follow the checklist on page 191 carefully. Notice that you are only required to use one of each element of style anywhere within all three paragraphs rather than one of each in every paragraph.

4. There are no new vocabulary words. Continue to review and use all.

Source Text

The samurai were the warrior class of feudal Japan. Similar to knights in Europe, they protected the lands of their lords. The following story is an old story often told to martial arts (karate) students in Japan. What lesson do you think the students should learn from it?

The Determined Samurai

retold by Lori Verstegen

Long ago in medieval Japan, a young samurai fell deeply in love. His sweetheart, Sayoko, loved him just as deeply. They planned to be married. One day as they strolled through the jungle, a vicious tiger sprang out from behind the trees and pounced on Sayoko. The samurai jumped on the tiger and wrestled with it until it finally fled away, but it was too late. His beloved was dead. From that day forward the young samurai swore revenge. He grabbed his bow and arrows and set out for the jungle to hunt the cruel beast. Day after day he searched until one day he was sure he had spotted it—and it was sleeping! It was his perfect chance. He drew his bow and with all his strength shot an arrow. The arrow pierced its target. However, when the samurai approached to claim his victim, he found that the arrow was stuck fast in a huge rock! When the villagers heard about this, they marveled at his strength, for who could drive an arrow into a rock? They wanted to see him repeat the feat, but no matter how hard he tried, he could not do it again. Arrow after arrow bounced off rock after rock. Soon he realized that it had only been his passionate resolve to avenge his loved one that had given him such power.

Notes for Story Sequence Chart
Students only need to describe the samurai and the tiger. Remind the students that the conflict is the desire of the main character, and the climax is the event that lets us know how his problem/desire will work out. In this story, the samurai desires to kill the tiger but never succeeds in that. When do we realize that he will not kill the tiger?

Lesson 27: "The Determined Samurai" (Theme Analysis)

The Story Sequence Chart

Introduction

Title, Author
Publisher, Date
Type of Story
Background

I. _"The Determined Samurai," retold, L. Verstegen_

1. _pub, IEW, 2015_

2. _moral, story_

3. _inspire, karate, students_

Story Sequence Chart

Describe each **character** and the **setting**.
What is the **conflict**? (What is the desire of the main character?)
What happens?
What is the **climax**? (When do you know how the conflict will end?)
What is the **result**?

II. _main, char, sam, yng, love, Japan_

1. _+ tiger, merciless, xx, beloved_

2. _conflict = sam, desires, revenge_

3. _hunts, tiger, shoots_

4. _climax, disc, shot, rock_

5. _result, ppl, marvel, strength_

6. _can't, repeat, b/c ↓ resolve_

Theme Analysis

What does the main character learn?
How? Explain the part of the story in which he learns the lesson.
What is the significance?
Can the lesson be applied to other people in different circumstances? How?
End with a final clincher that shows your opinion of the story and theme. Do not write *I* or *my*.

III. _sam, learns, w/resolve, strength_

1. _learns, b/c, Ø, repeat, pierce_

2. _knows, Ø, tiger, = ↓ desire_

3. _desire,= key ,success_

4. _many, pts, life, same_

5. _Ø force, ppl, do, Ø, want_

6. _want, enuf, find, way_

Concluding Statement

"Det. Sam," story, power, resolve

Unit 9: Response to Literature

The #5 Sentence Opener

Good writing should include a variety of sentence types and lengths. Thus far you have been purposely using three types of sentence openers to accomplish this: the #2 (prepositional), the #3 (-ly adverb), and the #4 (-ing opener). In this lesson you will learn to include a #5, a www.asia. because clause, as an opener as well.

Remember that a www.asia.b clause begins with one of these words: *when, while, where, as, since, if, although,* or *because.* You have been using this type of clause as a dress-up, but now you must use it as a sentence opener, too.

Remember, a www.asia.b cannot be a complete sentence by itself. (It is a dependent clause; it is dependent on more information to finish the thought.) The clause must be added to a sentence that is already complete. Look at the sample sentences in the box below. The www.asia.b clauses are the clauses that begin with one of the www.asia.b words.

If the clause is at the beginning of a sentence, it is a #5 opener, and a *5* indicates it in the left margin. It does not need to be underlined. Notice that a clause at the beginning of a sentence is followed by a comma. *Can you find a #5 opener in the sample anecdote on page 188?*

When the villagers heard about this ...

Sample Clauses

Notice how the clauses are indicated. Do the same when you use a www.asia.b clause in your writing.

5   When Sayoko is killed, the samurai swears to take revenge.

5   Although he tries hard to pierce the rock, his heart is not in it like before.

Notice that when you remove the www.asia.because word from each of the above sentences, you will be left with two complete sentences joined together.

Practice

Write a #5 sentence that could be in your composition. Remember to put a comma after the clause.

5   *As he grabbed his weapons, he stirred up his courage.*

Lesson 27: "The Determined Samurai" (Theme Analysis)

Lesson 27 Final Checklist -
"The Determined Samurai" (Theme Analysis)

FORMAT

☐ Modified MLA format (See Appendix 1.) _____ (3 pts)

STRUCTURE

☐ Title repeats or reflects key words from final clincher. _____ (3 pts)

☐ I. **Introduction**: title, author, publisher, background _____ (5 pts)

☐ II. **Characters/Setting** _____ (5 pts)

☐ **Conflict/Plot** _____ (5 pts)

☐ **Climax, Resolution** _____ (5 pts)

III. **Theme**

☐ Identify the theme. (What is learned?) _____ (5 pts)

☐ How is it learned? _____ (5 pts)

☐ Discuss the significance of the theme. _____ (5 pts)

☐ Final clincher reflects your opinion. _____ (5 pts)

STYLE Entire composition must contain at least one of each element of style.

Dress-Ups (Underline one of each; abbreviate in right margin.)   **(3 pts each)**

☐ -ly adverb _____ (3 pts)

☐ *who–which* clause _____ (3 pts)

☐ strong verb _____ (3 pts)

☐ quality adjective _____ (3 pts)

☐ www.asia.b clause _____ (3 pts)

Sentence Openers (numbered; one of each as possible)   **(3 pts each)**

☐ [2] prepositional _____ (3 pts)

☐ [3] -ly adverb _____ (3 pts)

☐ [4] -ing , _____ (3 pts)

☐ [5] clausal, www.asia.b _____ (3 pts)

Decoration (Use at least one per para.) ("dec" in margin or italics)   **(2 pts each)**

☐ alliteration, simile, or 3sss _____ (2 pts)

MECHANICS

☐ banned words: I, my, you, your _____ (-1 pt)

☐ banned words: go/went say/said nice/mean _____ (-1 pt)

MORE ADVANCED ADDITIONS

☐ vocabulary words (*Label voc or bold.*) _____

☐ dual adjective, verb, or -ly adverb _____

☐ triple extension _____

Total _____ /75

Custom total _____ / _____

Unit 9: Response to Literature

Institute for Excellence in Writing

Teachers, review Unit 8: Formal Essay in the TWSS workbook before teaching Lessons 28–30. If you have the seminar on DVD, watch the corresponding lesson.

Unit 8: Formal Essay with Library Research

Lesson 28: Renaissance Men

Review

You have adapted the basic essay model in several ways. What are the components of a basic 5-paragraph essay such as you would use for a report?

introduction, three body paragraphs, conclusion

In Lessons 28–30 you will write a research report. The basic 5-paragraph essay model such as you would use for a report has an introduction, three body paragraphs (each with its own topic), and a conclusion. This is like the knights report from Lessons 19, 20, and 25. You will use this same structure. However, for this report, you will need to find most of your own sources. Learning to find appropriate sources is a valuable skill to practice.

In the following three lessons, you will write about Renaissance men. Probably the easiest way to do this is to choose one discipline, such as art, and then choose three great men in that discipline. This lesson will suggest choosing Renaissance artists as your subject. One or two sources for each suggested artist is provided for you. You will need to find at least two other sources. History textbooks, Internet articles (especially those googled "for kids"), encyclopedia articles, and short children's books will make the best sources. Your parents or a librarian should help you choose short, easy sources. The difficulty of this essay will be determined largely by the difficulty of the sources you use.

Choosing Topics

The subject of your essay has been assigned. The first step in writing your research report is to familiarize yourself with the subject by gathering sources and scanning them. Your goal in this is to determine three topics. Source 1 on page 195 will give you a general overview of the Renaissance. Sources 2–4 provide at least one source for each of the suggested artists to serve as your topics:

    A. Leonardo da Vinci

    B. Michelangelo

    C. Raphael

However, you are free to choose other Renaissance men as topics if you like. *The Medieval History-Based Advanced Lessons Blackline Masters* provide sources for Renaissance scientists: Copernicus and Galileo.

Regardless of which Renaissance men you choose to write about, you must begin with Leonardo da Vinci, as he is known as "the Ultimate Renaissance Man" and was an artist and a scientist and so much more.

Once you have determined your other topics, follow the assignment instructions on the next page.

Unit 8: Formal Essay with Library Research

The Assignment

Day 1:

1. Read Source 1, page 195, to familiarize yourself with the Renaissance.

2. Prepare a sheet of paper like page 198 for Topic A. Take notes on this paper for a paragraph about Leonardo da Vinci since he is required to be the first topic. Read both Source 2 and Source 3 (pages 196–197) to get your notes. Remember that you must limit the number of facts you write. Choose only what is most interesting or most important.

3. Use page 199 to fuse your notes into an outline for one paragraph about da Vinci. This is the outline from which you will write your paragraph.

4. Be sure to go over instructions for Days 2–4.

Days 2–4:

1. Polish the "Genghis Khan and His Hawk" essay from Lesson 26.

2. Use the fused outline you wrote in class to write one paragraph about Leonardo da Vinci as a Renaissance artist.

3. Repeat Steps 2–3 of Day 1 to take notes and make a fused outline for a second Renaissance man. If you will write about Michelangelo, use Source 4, page 200, as one of your sources.

   Important: You must find a second or third source of your own for this topic. Look for short texts such as in a history book, an encyclopedia article, or an Internet article. Write the titles and authors of the sources above the notes you take from them. Save the sources because they must be added to a bibliography later.

   You do not need to fill in every line of the notes. When reading your second and third source, you may only find one or two new facts. That is okay. You do not need to rewrite facts you already noted from a previous source.

4. Use your fused outline to write one paragraph about Michelangelo (or the substitute Renaissance man of your choice). Follow the checklist on page 207. (You will write the remaining paragraph on the checklist next week.)

Important: Bring at least two sources for your Topic C to class next week.

Literature Suggestion

With Lessons 28–31 read *Crispin: The Cross of Lead* by Avi.

Source 1

The Renaissance
by Lori Verstegen

The end of the Middle Ages merged into a period of history known as the Renaissance. The term *Renaissance* comes from a Latin word meaning *rebirth*. During this time period, scholars and artists sought to return to the spirit of the Greek and Roman cultures that had valued the arts and learning. The Renaissance began in Italy in the 1300s and slowly spread throughout Europe. As a result, Europe experienced remarkable advances, especially in the arts and sciences. Most scholars agree that our modern era began with the Renaissance.

The influence of Renaissance painters, sculptors, and architects has been particularly enduring. Renaissance artists such as Leonardo da Vinci, Michelangelo, and Raphael desired to portray man and nature realistically. They experimented with perspective, color, light, and shading to achieve great masterpieces. They set a new standard for art. Renaissance architects such as Brunelleschi used Roman and Greek architecture as their inspiration; thus, many Renaissance buildings included columns and arches. Italy especially is world-renowned for its glorious Renaissance works of architecture and art. They are still studied today.

Renaissance scientists, inventors, and explorers also made great advances that had far-reaching effects. During the Renaissance, scientists began to challenge ancient teachings that had been commonly accepted for centuries. For example, Copernicus challenged the idea that the earth was the center of the universe. He proposed a sun-centered model. In addition, many devices were invented that helped great thinkers experiment and explore. For example, the telescope helped scientists study the heavens. With it Galileo made many new discoveries about the solar system. Also, Gutenberg's printing press made it possible to share ideas and knowledge on a much grander scale. Men were inspired to explore the world and the universe. Some of the greatest explorers of the 1400s and 1500s, such as Christopher Columbus, were Italians exposed to the ideas of Renaissance thinkers. The world was forever changed by the men of the Renaissance.

As you read through each source the first time, have students underline things they think are essential. Help them limit their choices and focus on main ideas.

Unit 8: Formal Essay with Library Research

Source 2

Leonardo da Vinci
by Chelsea M.

Leonardo da Vinci was born in the small town of Vinci on April 15, 1452. He is one of the greatest painters of all time. However, he was not only a marvelous painter, but also an ingenious inventor, a brilliant scientist, a cunning military engineer, a botanist, and a mathematician.

As a child, Leonardo had very little education. At the age of 14, he was apprenticed to a great artist in Florence named Verrocchio. While under Verrocchio's care, Leonardo learned many workshop skills. He was taught painting, sculpting, drafting, metalworking, plaster casting, and carpentry. One day Verrocchio asked Leonardo to paint an angel in the painting *The Baptism of Christ* that they were working on. When Verocchio saw how skillfully Leonardo had painted the angel, he put his brush down and swore never to paint again.

Leonardo had a passion to portray things as realistically as possible. He sketched incessantly and studied animals, plants, and people intently. He went to hospitals to watch operations and visited morgues to dissect bodies in order to understand human anatomy. As a painter, he is best known for his ability to use shadows and light to achieve perspective and depth. This is evident in the painting he is best known for, *The Mona Lisa*. This painting of an unknown woman has intrigued the world for centuries. Her mysterious smile and eyes that seem to follow observers no matter where they stand make this painting the most famous painting in history. *The Last Supper* is another of Leonardo's famous paintings. It took him three years to complete. This painting depicts Jesus in the Upper Room with his disciples. He has just told them that one of them will betray him. Shock and horror can be seen on the disciple's faces. This beautiful work of art is the most reproduced painting of all time. Truly, Leonardo da Vinci is one of the greatest painters who ever lived.

Source 3

The Ultimate Renaissance Man
by Lori Verstegen

Leonardo da Vinci has often been called "the ultimate Renaissance Man" because he had so many interests and talents. In fact, he may have been the most multi-talented person to have ever lived. He studied anatomy, astronomy, botany, and geology. In addition, he sketched plans for hundreds of machines and inventions ahead of his time, like a flying machine and a parachute.

However, Leonardo was trained to be a painter, and that is what he is most remembered for. In the 1460s, while just a boy, he was apprenticed to Andrea del Verrocchio, a prominent painter and sculptor in Florence. Leonardo helped Verrocchio paint *The Baptism of Christ*. From 1478–1482, Leonardo had his own studio but never finished an important work there. He moved to Milan to be the court artist for the Duke. There he painted the earliest of his works that has survived in complete form: *Madonna on the Rocks*. He worked hard to make his paintings look real. He gave them depth and correct proportion, unlike the paintings of his day that were flat and out of proportion. In Milan he also painted one of his most famous works, *The Last Supper*, on the wall of a monastery. Leonardo developed his own technique for this painting. He wanted to be able to work slowly and carefully to make it realistic. However, the scene soon faded and began to flake. *The Last Supper*, which is a true masterpiece, has had to be restored many times and is still in poor condition.

In 1499, Leonardo returned to Florence. There he painted what is perhaps the most recognized painting of all time: the *Mona Lisa*. In this painting of a woman with a mysterious smile, Leonardo broke from the traditional method of painting portraits, which was to show only the head and chest, because this made the subjects look cut off. Leonardo included the woman's hands folded on her lap. This gave her a more complete, natural appearance.

In his later years. Leonardo did not paint much but, instead, sketched many ideas for inventions that became some of his most famous works. In 1517, he moved to France at the request of the king, who wanted to have famous men of the Renaissance in his land. Leonardo died near Tours, France, two years later.

Teach students to underline titles of paintings (and other artwork) when writing KWOs. When typing, they should be italicized.

Unit 8: Formal Essay with Library Research

Key Word Outlines - Renaissance Men *(Take notes on your own paper, following this format.)*

Topic A: Leonardo da Vinci

Source 2: "Leonardo da Vinci" by M. (page 196)

1. born, Vinci, 1452

2. 1, > pntrs, ever

3. @14 apprent, Verrochio, Florence

4. angel, <u>Baptism of Christ</u>, > skillfully

5. ➔ Verr, swore, ⊘ paint

6. passion, realistically, w/depth

7. best, known, <u>Mona Lisa</u>

8. + <u>Last Supper</u>, 3 yrs, most, reproduced

Source 3: "The Ultimate Renaissance Man" by Verstegen (page 197)

1. > talents, remem, painter

2. moved, Milan, artist, Dk

3. earliest, survived: <u>Madonna on the Rocks</u>

4. worked, depth, proportion

5. + <u>Last Supper</u>, monastery, wall

6. 1999, rtn, Florence, <u>Mona Lisa</u>

7. <u>unique</u>, view, w/lap

8. 1517, ➔ France, XX, Tours, 1519

Institute for Excellence in Writing

Fused Outline

Choose facts from the notes you took from all sources for Topic A: Leonardo da Vinci. Put them in an order that makes sense.

I. Topic A: _Leonardo da Vinci, 1 > pntrs, ever_

    1. _born, Vinci, 1452_

    2. _@14, ➜ Florence, appren, Verrochio_

    3. _angel, Baptism of Christ, skillfully_

    4. _➜, Verr, swore, ⊘ paint_

    5. _passion, pnt, realistically_

    6. _w/depth + correct, proportion_

    7. _Mona Lisa, most, recognized_

    8. _Last Supper, 3yrs, monastery, wall_

    9. _most, repro, pntg, ever_

Clincher A

Source 4 for Topic B

A Magnificent Artist
by Izzy

Michelangelo was born in 1475 and died in 1564. He is best known for his sculptures and fresco paintings; however, he was also an architect and a poet. Like Leonardo da Vinci, he analyzed the human body for many years, which gave him the ability to sculpt realistically. One of his most famous sculptures is *David*. This 17-foot-tall marble statue is perfectly designed in exact proportion. He also sculpted the *Pieta*, which is a sculpture of Mary holding Jesus after the crucifixion. In addition, Pope Julius II asked Michelangelo to sculpt for his tomb. A statue of *Moses* is at the center of the tomb. This was Michelangelo's last major sculpture. While he was an excellent sculptor, Michelangelo is probably most famous for his paintings in the Sistine Chapel. On the ceiling there are scenes of creation, Adam and Eve, and the flood. The edges of the ceiling have seven prophets and five sibyls (female prophets). At the rear of the chapel there is a painting of *The Last Judgment*. Because he was so admired in his time, he was called "Il Divino" (the Divine One). His sculptures and paintings still amaze people. Michelangelo was a magnificent Renaissance artist.

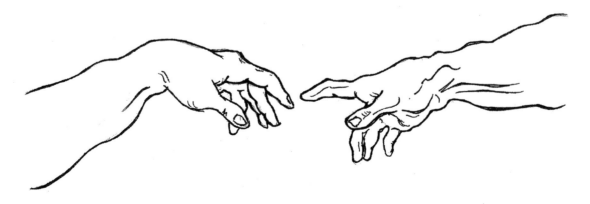

Key Word Outlines - Renaissance Men *(Take notes on your own paper, following this format.)*

Topic B: Michelangelo (or substitute topic of your choice)

Source: "A Magnificent Artist" by Izzy (page 200)

1. *born, 1475, XX, 1564*

2. *fam, sculpt, + fresco, pntgs*

3. *analyzed, human, ➔ realistic*

4. *> fam, sculp, <u>David</u>, 17 ft, marble, = proport*

5. *<u>Pieta</u>, Mary, w/Jesus, ⬇, cross*

6. *<u>Moses</u>, Pope Julius's, tomb*

7. *renowned, pntg, Sistine Chapel*

8. *scenes, ceiling, walls*

Source:

1. *Each student will take notes from his or her own source here.*

2.

3.

4.

(Optional) Source:

1.

2.

3.

4.

Unit 8: Formal Essay with Library Research

Fused Outline

Choose facts from the notes you took from all sources for Topic B. Put them in an order that makes sense.

II. Topic B: _Each student will fuse notes from his or her own sources._

1. _____

2. _____

3. _____

4. _____

5. _____

6. _____

7. _____

Clincher B

(Checklist is on page 207.)

Institute for Excellence in Writing

If students are writing about different men and using different sources, taking notes together in class is not practical. Check to see that the sources they brought are at an appropriate level. Remind them to use the format for note taking on page 202. You may have your students work independently in class where you can help them, or you can assign the note taking, fused outline, and paragraph for homework. In that case, use class time to play a review game (21 Questions) with the questions on pages 282–283. Use questions 15–37.

Unit 8: Formal Essay with Library Research

Lesson 29 Renaissance Men, continued

Review

1. What is the structure of the 5-paragraph research report we are working on?

---

introduction paragraph, three body paragraphs, conclusion paragraph

---

2. Read the topic sentence and clincher of each of the two body paragraphs you wrote last week.

The Assignment

Day 1: Topic C

1. Prepare a sheet of paper like page 204. Take notes from at least two sources on this paper for a paragraph about your third Renaissance man. If you will do Raphael, you may use the source on page 206 as one source. Take notes for this together in class.

Days 2–4

1. Polish your "The Determined Samurai" composition from Lesson 27.

2. Finish taking notes from at least two sources about your third Renaissance man.

3. Use page 205 to fuse your notes into an outline for one paragraph on Topic C. This is the outline from which you will write your paragraph.

4. Use your fused outline to write one paragraph about Topic C. Add this paragraph to the two you wrote last week.

5. Follow the checklist on page 207.

Important: Bring all of the sources you used for this report to class next week.

Unit 8: Formal Essay with Library Research

Key Word Outlines - Renaissance Men *(Take notes on your own paper, following this format.)*

Topic C:

Source: "Raphael of the High Renaissance" by H. and Verstegen

1. *1483–1520, of , High Ren*

2. *fam, color, clarity, proportion*

3. *studied, da Vinci, Michelangelo*

4. *Michel, "everything from me"*

5. *> pieces, Vatican, (pope's HQ)*

6. *ex: School of Athens, framed, w/arch*

7. *w/Gk, phil, honor, love, learning*

8. *XX, @37, 100s, paintings*

Source:

1. *Each student will take notes from his or her own source here.*

2.

3.

4.

(Optional) Source:

1.

2.

3.

4.

Fused Outline

Choose facts from the notes you took from all sources for Topic C. Put them in an order that makes sense.

III. Topic C: *Each student will fuse notes from his or her own sources.*

1. _____

2. _____

3. _____

4. _____

5. _____

6. _____

7. _____

Clincher C

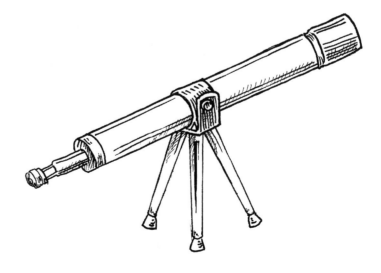

Unit 8: Formal Essay with Library Research

Source Text for Topic C

Raphael of the High Renaissance
by Madison H. and Lori Verstegen

Raphael, who lived from 1483 to 1520, was an Italian artist of the High Renaissance. He is famous for his use of color, clarity, and proportion. At age eleven, he was sent to Perugino, an important painter who greatly influenced Raphael's style. Raphael also studied the paintings of the renowned Italian artists Leonardo da Vinci and Michelangelo. In fact, Michelangelo complained that everything Raphael knew about art he had learned from him. Raphael painted altarpieces, frescoes (painted into the plaster of a wall), and portraits. Early in his career he painted a series of Madonnas (pictures of the Virgin Mary with Christ as a baby). In the year 1508, Pope Julius II requested that Raphael work for him in Rome. The pope desired to redecorate Rome to reflect its ancient glory. When Raphael was in Rome, he designed the new St. Peter's Basilica. Some of his greatest pieces of art are his frescoes in the Vatican, the pope's own headquarters. An example of this would be the *School of Athens*. Cleverly, he used the arch of the wall to frame it. This masterpiece sums up the Renaissance love for ancient learning as it shows Plato, Aristotle, and many of the great ancient Greek philosophers. Sadly, Raphael died at only thirty-seven years of age, but in spite of his short life, he left hundreds of paintings for the world to enjoy. Raphael is one of the greatest artists of the High Renaissance.

Lesson 28–29 Final Checklist (Body Paragraphs) - Renaissance Men

FORMAT

☐ Modified MLA format (See Appendix 1.)   _____ (3 pts)

STRUCTURE

☐ ☐ ☐ Each paragraph has a topic sentence (key words highlighted).   _____ (6 pts)

☐ ☐ ☐ Each paragraph has a clincher.
(Words reflected from the topic sentence are highlighted.)   _____ (6 pts)

STYLE Each paragraph must contain at least one of each element of style.

¶ A	¶ B	¶ C	Dress-Ups (Underline one of each; abbreviate in right margin.)	(2 pts each)
☐	☐	☐	-ly adverb	_____ (6 pts)
☐	☐	☐	*who–which* clause	_____ (6 pts)
☐	☐	☐	strong verb	_____ (6 pts)
☐	☐	☐	quality adjective	_____ (6 pts)
☐	☐	☐	www.asia.b clause	_____ (6 pts)

			Sentence Openers (numbered; one of each as possible)	(2 pts each)
☐	☐	☐	[2] prepositional	_____ (6 pts)
☐	☐	☐	[3] -ly adverb	_____ (6 pts)
☐	☐	☐	[4] -ing ,	_____ (6 pts)
☐	☐	☐	[5] clausal, www.asia.b	_____ (6 pts)

			Decorations (Use at least one per para.) ("dec" in margin or italics)	(2 pts each)
☐	☐	☐	alliteration, simile, or 3sss	_____ (6 pts)

MECHANICS

☐ banned words: go/went say/said nice/mean   _____ (-1 pt)

MORE ADVANCED ADDITIONS

☐ vocabulary words (*Label voc or bold.*)   _____

☐ dual adjective, verb, or -ly adverb   _____

☐ triple extension   _____

Total _____ /75

Custom total _____ / _____

Unit 8: Formal Essay with Library Research

Unit 8: Formal Essay with Library Research

Lesson 30: Renaissance Men, Final

Now that you have finished the body of your research report, you must add the introduction, conclusion, and a bibliography. To do so, follow the assignment instructions below.

The Assignment

Day 1

1. With your teacher, fill out the outlines on page 211 for the introduction and conclusion of the Renaissance Men research report. Use page 210 for help.

2. After you outline each, read over your notes, and tell back the information in complete sentences to be sure you understand your notes and connect the ideas smoothly.

3. Begin your bibliography. See pages 212–213.

Days 2–4

1. Use your introduction outline on page 211 to write and add an introduction to the beginning of your research report.

2. Use your conclusion outline on page 211 to write and add a conclusion to the end of your research report.

3. Complete your bibliography. (See pages 212–213.)

4. Put the entire research report together. Follow and attach both checklists: pages 207 and 214.

Introduction

Grab attention:	Begin with a statement that will grab your reader's interest. What do you believe is the most interesting thing about the Renaissance? (You could try the very short sentence dramatic opener here if you like. Review page 173.)
Subject and background:	What was the Renaissance? When and where was the Renaissance? What was important about it? For help with background, see Source 1 on page 195.
Topics:	Mention each of your three topics. Telling what each man is best known for is a possible way to do this. Another idea is to list them in a sentence that tells what they all, as a group, are renowned for.

Conclusion

Reflect topics:	Again, mention each of the three men.
Most significant:	What is the most important thing about Renaissance men? Do not choose one man. What was special about all of them?
Why?	What did the most significant thing result in?
Final clincher:	Repeat or reflect 2–3 words from the beginning of the introduction.

Introduction

Attention grabber: *They, created, > masterpieces (This is a vss dramatic opener.)*

Subject and background: *Ren., artists, out, dark*

desire, realistic, ➜ techniques

realism, depth, proport, astounded

Topics: *A.   da Vinci, w/most fam, <u>Mona Lisa</u>*

B.   Michelangelo, Sistine, + sculpt

C.   Raphael, work, Vatican

Conclusion

Topics: *da Vinci, Michel, Raph, never, forgotten*

Most significant: *bold, changed, art, ∞*

Why?   *work + tech, still, ☺, studied*

mark, new, mod, era

Final clincher

Dramatic close (optional)

The Bibliography

The last page of a research report should be a bibliography. A bibliography lists all the sources you used to obtain your information. Turn to the Bibliography/Works Cited page in the SRN. That page explains how to do the bibliography.

Be sure to include, in alphabetical order, *all* of the sources you used. Note that for all sources, if no author is given, begin with the title of the article or book.

Note that article titles should be placed in quotation marks; book titles should be italicized or underlined.

For sources used from this book, since your teacher has a copy of the book, she may allow you to use the following format so that you only have to include one entry for all of these sources rather than a separate entry for each one.

Verstegen, Lori. *Medieval History-Based Writing Lessons*. Locust Grove: Institute for Excellence

in Writing, 2015. 195–206. Print.

Internet Articles

Internet articles can be tricky. If available, you must include not only the website, but the publisher of the website and the date posted. This information is sometimes difficult to find or not given at all. Look at the end of articles for the date posted. Sometimes that is also where you will find the author. Often you can also find the complete MLA citation there. Here is how to cite an Internet source:

Author's last name, first name. [If no author given, just skip this.] "Title of Article." [in quotes]

Title of website. [in italics] Publisher or Sponsor. [Put n.p. if not given.] Date posted.

[n.d. if not given.] Web. Date you looked at the site.

Here is a sample. Note that there is no author, so it begins with the title.

"Nicolaus Copernicus." *Bio.com.* A&E Television Networks, 2015. Web. 5 May 2015.

Rough Bibliography

Begin your bibliography in class where your teacher can help you.

1. Take out a clean sheet of paper. Write *Bibliography* on the center of the top line.

2. Take out the sources you brought from home, and stack them in alphabetical order by the authors' last names. If no author is given for some, use the first word of the title, other than *A, An, The*. (If the title is the first word of your entry, move these words to the end. For example, if "The Great One" is an article with no author, you would list it as "Great One, The" so that it is alphabetized by "Great.")

3. Using the SRN and page 212, begin a rough bibliography. Place the entry for this book (below) in the correct spot alphabetically if you used the sources in this book.

Bibliography

Verstegen, Lori. *Medieval History-Based Writing Lessons*. Locust Grove: Institute for

Excellence in Writing, 2015. 195–206. Print.

Unit 8: Formal Essay with Library Research

Lesson 30 Final Checklist -
Renaissance Men: Introduction and Conclusion

FORMAT

☐ Modified MLA format (See Appendix 1.) _____ (2 pts)

STRUCTURE

☐ Title repeats or reflects key words from final clincher. _____ (2 pts)

   I.   Introduction

☐   Grab attention _____ (2 pts)

☐   Subject and background info _____ (5 pts)

☐   Topics mentioned *(Label A, B, C.)* _____ (6 pts)

☐   Any four dress-ups, one dec., and three openers _____ (7 pts)

   V.   **Conclusion**

☐   Restate topics. *(Label A, B, C.)* _____ (6 pts)

☐   Any four dress-ups, one dec., and three openers _____ (7 pts)

☐   Most significant and why _____ (5 pts)

☐   Final clincher *(Circle words that reflect the opening.)* _____ (2 pts)
    (If you used a dramatic vss opener, add a dramatic closer.)

MECHANICS

☐ banned words: go/went say/said nice/mean _____ (-1 pt)

   Bibliography

☐   Alphabetical order _____ (2 pts)

☐   At least two outside sources (not from this book) _____ (2 pts)

☐   Entries formatted correctly _____ (2 pts)

MORE ADVANCED ADDITIONS

☐ vocabulary words *(Label voc or bold.)* _____

☐ dual adjective, verb, or -ly adverb _____

☐ triple extension _____

Total _____ /50

Custom total _____ / _____

Remember to attach the checklist for the body paragraphs (page 207).

Just for Fun

Lesson 31: Vocabulary Story

Vocabulary Story

Toward the end of the year, I like to have a "just for fun" assignment. My classes have always enjoyed writing vocabulary stories. Not only are they a fun way to end the year, but they serve as a great review of the vocabulary words you have learned.

The instructions are simple: write a story using as many vocabulary words as you can. You may write a familiar story (such as an Aesop fable or fairy tale), or make up your own story using the Story Sequence Chart as a guide. (View page 46 of this book, or look in the SRN.) There are only two rules:

1. Words must be used correctly and fit naturally.

2. You may not put more than three adjectives in front of one noun.

There is no checklist for this assignment, but tickets will be given as follows:

-   1 ticket for each vocabulary word used well

-   3 tickets for each decoration used well

Read the sample story in the appendix, pages 250–252 to get the idea.

The Assignment

Day 1

1. Take out a piece of paper, and with the help of your teacher write a blank story sequence outline on it. This will make a good review of Unit 3.

2. With a partner discuss ideas for a story. Begin filling out the outline and discussing ideas for adding vocabulary words. Having the chart of vocabulary words, pages 260–261, in front of you will be helpful.

3. After you have written the outline, begin writing your story.

Days 2–4

1. Write your story, adding as many vocabulary words as you can. Bold each. Also, try to include five-senses words (highlight) and some decorations (label). These will make the story more enjoyable to read.

Just for Fun

Appendices

Appendices

Institute for Excellence in Writing

Appendix 1

Appendix 1: Modified MLA Format

1. Double-space the entire composition, including the heading and title. Set 1-inch margins all the way around.

2. Only the first page should have the heading in the upper left corner with your name, lesson number, and the date.

3. If your paper is more than one page, every page (including the first) must have a header in the top right corner with your last name and page number. Look at the sample below.

4. The text should be left justified. Use 12 pt Times New Roman or similar serif font. Paragraphs should be indented half an inch. There should only be one space after end punctuation to separate sentences.

Your essay should use the format shown below at 3/4 scale.

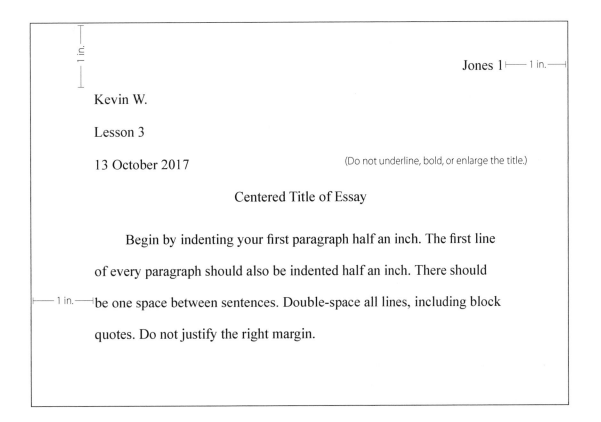

Appendix 1: Modified MLA Format

Teachers, you do not need to mark every error. Mark glaring errors and concepts that you have already taught or that they should be able to understand easily. Be sure to include positive feedback as well.

Appendix 2: Polished Draft Notebook and Keepsake

Students should polish and illustrate each of their final drafts as soon as they have been checked and returned by a teacher.

To polish a final draft, students should make the corrections noted. Parents should help their student understand the reason for each correction. This last draft is referred to as "the polished draft" and does not have to be labeled.

The following page is the checklist that should be attached to each polished draft if teachers require them to be turned in. To check, teachers simply make sure that each correction marked on the final draft has been made and that a picture has been added.

Once returned, polished drafts should be kept in a half-inch binder in clear sheet protectors *with the original, labeled final drafts hidden behind the first page of each.* At the end of the year, students will have a fine collection of a variety of types of compositions that move through major themes in medieval history.

Each student also may do an "About the Author" page as his title page. This can either be a paragraph about himself or an acrostic poem. For the poem option, each student writes his name in large, bold letters in a column down the page. He then uses each of the letters of his name as the first letter of each line of the poem describing himself. With either option, students include a picture of themselves.

Also, I make a picture collage of the class for each of the kids to put in the front of their notebooks. The kids also sign others' books on blank paper placed at the end of the notebook (like a year book) in a clear sheet protector.

All these things make the polished draft notebook a wonderful keepsake of the year.

In a class setting, I display the polished draft notebooks at the end of the year at our Parent Day party.

Important: Teachers should periodically require the students to bring their polished draft notebooks to class, so you can check that they are keeping up with them.

Make sixteen copies of this page. You will need one checklist for each lesson.

Polished Draft Checklist

Each item is worth 5 points.

- ☐ Polished draft is in clear sheet protector(s) with the original final draft and checklist hidden behind the first page.
- ☐ Composition is neat and double-spaced.
- ☐ Elements of style missing on final draft have been added.
- ☐ Grammar and spelling corrections have been made.
- ☐ Picture is added.
  (You may draw or you may cut and paste from the Internet.)

Note: Polished drafts do not have to be relabeled.

Total _____

Polished Draft Checklist

Each item is worth 5 points.

- ☐ Polished draft is in clear sheet protector(s) with the original final draft and checklist hidden behind the first page.
- ☐ Composition is neat and double-spaced.
- ☐ Elements of style missing on final draft have been added.
- ☐ Grammar and spelling corrections have been made.
- ☐ Picture is added.
  (You may draw or you may cut and paste from the Internet.)

Note: Polished drafts do not have to be relabeled.

Total _____

Appendix 3: Student Samples

This appendix is a collection of student samples for each of the IEW units. Most of these samples were chosen to reward students who did an outstanding job on the assignment. They should inspire your students to do their best. Please realize that most include the advanced lessons because I typically teach sixth through eighth grade students who possess higher skills.

Unit		Lesson	Title	Page
2	Summarizing	3	Angleland	224
2		4	The End of Beowulf	225
3	Story	6	With God All Things Are Possible	226
3	Borrowing a Conflict	10	Sir Braveone	229
3	Rhyming Story	10	The Dwarves' Lesson	231
4	Report	12–13	A Famous Ruler of Medieval Times	233
5	Pictures	17	The Dragon of Justice	235
6	Research	19–20	Juggernauts of the Middle Ages	238
7	Inventive	24	21st Century Magic	240
9	Critique	26	Tragedy Worth Remembering	243
9	Theme Analysis	27	The Power of Resolve	245
8	Essay	28–30	Great Men of the Renaissance	246
	Vocabulary Story	31	The Little Red Hen	250

UNIT 2 SAMPLE

Lesson 3: Anglo-Saxons

Leanne W.

Lesson 3

Sept. 16, 2013

Angleland

When the Roman Empire collapsed, Anglo-Saxons invaded Britain from the main continent of Europe. The Angles, as they were often called, were tribal people who settled in the south of Britain. They called this place Angleland, <u>which morphed into our current word England</u>. The Anglo-Saxons were the first men to speak English, so we have them to thank for the most popular language in the world today. They had many ups and downs; for example, they may have established the base for a great country that played a major role in the world, but they were <u>utterly</u> uncivilized. They also brought their pagan religion with them to the new land and were not **intrigued** at all by arts or science. The king of their gods, Woden, gave us the word Wednesday, which was derived from Woden's day. In AD 598, a Christian monk named Augustine **ventured*** into their land and converted many Angles to Christianity. The Anglo-Saxons ruled England until AD 1066, when they were conquered by the Normans.

****Note:** I encourage my students to use vocabulary words from past IEW classes as well as their current class. Ventured, which is in bold above, is from* All Things Fun and Fascinating.

UNIT 2 SAMPLE

Lesson 4: Beowulf (with Advanced Lessons)

Luke H.

Lesson 4

September 24, 2014

The End of Beowulf

A **massive** dragon slept for centuries under a humongous hill. As long as its hoard of   *dec.*

sparkling jewels, glittering gold, and shining coins was not disturbed, it would slumber. One day

a runaway slave, seeking shelter, discovered the cavern. He was **stunned** at the sight of the piles

of treasure but at the same time was terrified at the sight of the scaly dragon. He at once fled the

cave but first <u>greedily</u> took a great, golden goblet. The bulky beast, awakened, acutely heard the   *dec., 2x*

slave's noises and realized his goblet was missing. He aroused himself and **pursued** the **fleeing**

slave. When he was unable to locate the slave, he instead set fire to the surrounding villages.

Burnt buildings blazed with orange light as the dragon **dilapidated** the villages. After having his

fill of carnage, the dragon returned to its damp cavern.

Though Beowulf, <u>now a king</u>, was old, he knew he had to eliminate the dragon. He left to

kill the monster. Fire seared from the mouth of the dragon's cave. Beowulf **<u>intrepidly</u>** challenged

the dragon to **emerge*** from his cave, and the dragon appeared, **quaking*** the ground and roaring

deafeningly with its **fetid** breath. The two met and fought. Beowulf fought with his sword and

glinting shield and the dragon with its pointed teeth and claws. All of Beowulf's men ran at sight

of the dragon except the youngest, who stood to assist his king. Beowulf's sword broke, and the

dragon grasped him by his neck. The soldier who had stayed climbed the beast and stabbed its

neck until it released Beowulf. Then the two hacked at the dragon's neck until it collapsed. The

rest of the country was saved though King Beowulf was mortally wounded.

*These words are from a previous IEW class (Ancient History-Based).

Appendix 3: Student Samples

UNIT 3 SAMPLE

Lesson 6: Augustine (with Advanced Lessons)

Arielle A.

Lesson 6

12 November 2013

With God All Things Are Possible

In sixth-century Rome Pope Gregory <u>briskly</u> walked through the town square, <u>which</u> was only about half full with people due to the recent weather. Pope Gregory looked at the dreary sky and a drop of cold rain hit his face. Pope Gregory continued walking through the square when it started to hail, so he ducked underneath the nearest canvas. *The slave market, just my luck*, he thought. Pope Gregory could hear the lash of the whip and the cry of brothers and sisters, mothers and daughters, fathers and sons being separated, while above it all, there was the auctioneer smiling and rattling off prices to the rich, lazy crowd. *Do they have no sympathy?* he wondered. As he **ventured** closer, he looked at the line of slaves. In the midst of all the others there were three young boys. These boys looked very different, though. They had white skin and golden hair. Pope Gregory, being kind and curious, decided to buy the boys, but first he had to find the person in charge.

"Pope! What are you doing here? I told you I am not going to shut down my business!" the slave master yelled.

"That isn't why I'm here. I would like to buy those three," he explained, pointing to the boys.

"Ah! Those three! Now that, I am afraid, will cost you extra. You see, it's not often we get such odd things as these."

"They aren't things. They're human beings," the pope responded as he paid the trader.

"Take them!" the slave master bellowed.

Pope Gregory began to walk over to the ex-slaves when he turned and whispered, "There is still hope for you yet, Tomas. If you would only…"

"LEAVE!" Tomas shrieked.

So Pope Gregory turned, took the boys, and left.

Once Pope Gregory and the three boys arrived at the priory, it was seven in the evening.

"So," Pope Gregory asked, "What are your names?"

"My name is Andrew," declared the oldest, who looked to be about 13 years of age. "And these are my brothers, Peter and James."

"Hello," whispered the youngest, who was James.

"Hello, James," smiled Pope Gregory.

"Where are our parents?" worried Peter.

"Peter, I am sorry. I don't know where your parents are. But God does. If God wills it, you and your parents will be together soon," Pope Gregory assured.

"Who's God?" Andrew asked.

At this Pope Gregory was deeply saddened. "Where are you from, child?"

"Britain," the boy replied.

That night while the boys were sleeping, Pope Gregory sent for Augustine.

"Augustine, I have a very important job for you. I want you to go to Britain to teach the people there about God."

"Am I to go alone?" Augustine asked.

"No, take 40 brothers with you. I have a ship making ready."

"I will leave **presently**," replied Augustine, <u>who</u> had a heart for sharing his faith.

So Augustine and 40 monks set sail for Britain to tell its people about the Lord.

———————————

After many long weeks the ship and its passengers arrived in Britain. They <u>immediately</u> set out to find the king, Ethelbert.

"What do you want?" the king questioned.

"We have come here from Rome," replied Augustine. "And we want to tell your people about the Lord."

"Hmmm," thought the king, "my wife is a Christian. Very well, you may teach my people of God."

"Thank you sir," replied Augustine, <u>who</u> was a bit **stunned** by so quick a response. At first the people were confused by the teachings. As they began to understand, more and more people were converted until they were almost all Christians! In fact, on Christmas A.D. 597 they baptized thousands of people. As the years went on, the Pope sent more and more monks. They built churches all over southern England. Augustine was made archbishop and was called the apostle of England. This just shows that with God on your side anything is possible.

UNIT 3 SAMPLE

Lesson 10: Borrowing a Conflict

Daniel O.

Lesson 10

19 February 2010

Sir Braveone

In Ataland, by the **serene** Lake of Desire, there lived a **renowned** king with his three beautiful, **devout** daughters. Beyond the **massive** castle walls were four knights, <u>who</u> were raised to defend the land. However, Sir Lazyone sat on the couch all day and dreamed about **ravishing** damsels. Sir Busyone spend all day **<u>embellishing</u>** and shining his armor until it sparkled like the *dec.* stars. Sir Vainone enjoyed staring at himself <u>incessantly</u> in the mirror, fixing his **impeccable** hair this way and that. But Sir Braveone, <u>because</u> he was **intrepid**, rescued all the fair maidens in the kingdom.

There were many damsels in distress in Ataland, <u>especially</u> the king's three beautiful daughters <u>because</u> they were so highly desired. The king's first daughter, <u>Lady Beautifulone</u>, was held **interminably** captive in the top of a **vacant** tower, **stymied** by a **devious** king. Sir Braveone asked, "Who will help me save Lady Beautifulone?"

"Not I," replied Sir Lazyone.

"Not I," replied Sir Busyone.

"Not I," replied Sir Vainone.

"Then I will," <u>pledged</u> Sir Braveone. And he did.

The next day the king's second daughter, <u>Lady Faithfulone</u>, was <u>cornered</u> by a **<u>fetid</u>**, *dec.* <u>ferocious, fire-breathing</u> dragon. Sir Braveone **bellowed**, "Who will help me save Lady Faithfulone?"

Appendix 3: Student Samples

"Not I," replied Sir Lazyone.

"Not I," replied Sir Busyone.

"Not I," replied Sir Vainone.

"Then I will," <u>vowed</u> Sir Braveone. And he did.

The next day, the king's third daughter, Lady Fairone, was <u>cruelly</u> dragged away by an evil, **tenacious** knight. Sir Braveone yelled, "Who will help me save Lady Fairone?"

"Not I," replied Sir Lazyone.

"Not I," replied Sir Busyone.

"Not I," replied Sir Vainone.

"Then I will," promised Sir Braveone. And he did.

<u>Imminently</u> the king held a grand banquet to procure a suitor of his eldest daughter. Sir Lazyone jumped off the couch and rushed to the banquet. Sir Busyone dropped his armor and <u>stormed</u> to the castle. Sit Vainone turned from the mirror and paraded to the banquet. Sir Braveone was already there, making certain the king's young beautiful daughters were safe. When the king entered the banquet hall, he asked, "Who will marry Lady Beautifulone?"

"I will," volunteered Sir Lazyone.

"I will," **pleaded** Sir Busyone.

"I will," announced Sir Vainone.

But the king **extolled**, "<u>Because</u>, all by himself, Sir Braveone toiled to rescue Lady Beautifulone from the devious king, Lady Faithfulone from the fire-breathing dragon, and Lady Fairone from the evil knight, all by himself he shall marry Lady Beautifulone. And he did. After that, whenever there were damsels in distress in need of being rescued, Sir Braveone had three knights <u>who</u> were eager to help him.

Unit 3

Lesson 10: Poem (with Advanced Lessons)

Luke H.

Lesson 10

17 November 2014

The Dwarves' Lesson

Three **intrepid** dwarves left their dull home.

They <u>forged</u> a path and began to roam.

They found a huge cave with immense treasure

And stole its spoils with giddy pleasure.

Off they skipped on separate roads

To hide their money in new abodes.

Little did they know, a dragon lived there.

He awoke and found his bank account bare.

He roared in **despair** when he saw dwarf tracks

'<u>Cause</u> dwarves keep their plunder close to their backs.

The first dwarf, Snooze, built a **disclosed** wooden door

Then lay down on his wealth and began to snore

The next dwarf, Potato Chips, built a tent with metal pegs

And <u>happily</u> started to cook some sausage and eggs.

The third dwarf, Steve E., built a stone **fortress**, as was his vision,

Then installed a monitor and watched television.

Appendix 3: Student Samples

The **massive** dragon with bright blue scales   *dec.*

Searched high and low in the <u>valleys and vales</u>

Then he found those dwarves in a peaceful clearing

And soared down with his tail rearing

The dragon found Snooze sleeping

Until that fiery lizard sent him <u>screeching</u>.

Snooze ran with his coins as he ran almost tripping

To his brother, Potato Chips, <u>who</u> was nacho dipping.   *dec.*

Then the two cowered in their <u>puny pavilion</u>

While the dragon attacked with his eyes flashing cyan.

The brothers ran carrying gold with a few falls,

And luckily sprinted behind Steve E.'s rock walls.

The dragon tore open those obsidian doors with **haste**

Then pillaged the money and put it back its place.

The dwarves stood horrified on the open floor

They learned their lesson and stole no more.

Could the lesson be, "Don't store any earthly possession?"

Or is it, "Never steal from a dragon, or you'll live in regression?"

UNIT 4 SAMPLE

Lessons 12–13: Charlemagne (with Advanced Lessons)

Olivia C.

Lessons 12–13

10 Dec. 2012

A Famous Ruler of Medieval Times

The most <u>prominent</u> **ruler** of medieval times was **Charlemagne**. Charlemagne was

Europe's greatest conqueror during the Middle Ages. His name means "Charles the Great." After

his father and brother died, Charlemagne <u>inherited</u> the kingdom of the Franks, <u>which</u> is known

today as France and part of Germany. He was known to be kindhearted and religious. However,

when a battle approached him, he was a **ruthless** warrior. Charlemagne was eager to expand the

Frankish Kingdom, and he craved to spread Christianity throughout Europe. He <u>definitely</u> ruled

"by the sword and by the cross." Finally in 800, after 30 years of bloody wars, Charlemagne's

empire had increased to cover a **massive** amount of Western Europe. There had not been an

empire as immense as this since ancient Rome had **dilapidated**. Because he controlled so much

of the continent, Charlemagne, the great conqueror, was called the "Father of Europe."

The **devout** Charlemagne felt a great need to **reform** his empire <u>because</u> he worried

that his people were ignoring the importance of education and their dedication to the Lord. So

Charlemagne created laws for his kingdom. No matter how rich or poor the people were, they

had to attend church. Charlemagne paid a great amount of money to the monks to copy the Holy

Book. He then <u>ordered</u> roads and bridges to be built so that the priests could travel about more

easily and preach the gospel. Most <u>importantly</u>, he established schools all over his territory. The

most elaborate and prestigious school was in his very own palace. In addition, Charlemagne

entrusted immense amounts of land to his most faithful men, <u>who</u> kept it maintained and protected. This was the beginning of the system of knights. For the next 400 years, this structure of the European government was known as feudalism. Charlemagne is **renowned** for producing <u>vast</u> improvements to the great European empire.

As the founder of the Holy Roman Empire, Charlemagne influenced Christianity and was known as the Church's defender. He even protected Pope Leo III from brutal rebels <u>who</u> wanted to harm him. One Christmas Day, when Charlemagne was 60 years of age, he traveled to Rome to attend service at St. Peter's Basilica. As he was kneeling down to pray, Pope Leo III <u>silently</u> crept up and placed a jeweled crown on Charlemagne's head. Right then and there he pronounced him "Emperor of the Romans." Even though Charlemagne knew this would give him no more power than he already had, he <u>accepted</u> this treasure with gratefulness because it was a symbol of their support of each other. This made him even more determined to cease pagan worship all throughout Europe. From then on, Charlemagne was known as the founder of the Holy Roman Empire. **"Charles the Great"** was the most famous **ruler** of medieval Europe.

UNIT 5 SAMPLE

Lesson 17

Olivia C.

Lesson 17

11 February 2013

The Dragon of Justice

King Lambert sat on his regal, royal throne, **bewildered** and discouraged. He had no *dec., 2x*

idea what to do to save his kingdom. Last night, while he was enjoying the damp, dark evening *dec., 2x*

on his garnished balcony, he startlingly spotted a dragon soaring overhead. King Lambert stared

dumbfounded at the sight, until the dragon landed in an open field and bounded toward an

abandoned cave. Alarmed, the king assumed that the dragon intended to destroy his kingdom,

which was helpless. Because he was sickly and elderly, the king did not know what to do until *2x*

an idea suddenly popped into his head. Of course! Why hadn't he thought of it before? He would

post signs in the surrounding towns and offer a rich reward to anyone who could defeat this *dec.*

monstrous dragon. Immediately, he had the signs prepared and delivered. All that the king had to

do now was recline on his throne and wait.

The next morning, a young lad named Albert was sauntering through the bustling town

when he spied the posters. Instantly, he dashed toward the castle gates. He told his purpose to the

guards and was lead to the king's chamber.

"So, you have come to defeat the dragon, have you?" asked the king, who was resting on

his velvet couch.

"Yes, your majesty, I have," Albert replied.

"You look a wee bit young to be slaying a mighty dragon," the king chuckled.

"I am nimble and have been on many voyages. Now, do you want the dragon defeated or not?" challenged Albert.

The king gave in and directed Albert to the cave where the dragon made his home. Albert advanced toward the cave **clad** in only a heavy helmet for protection. **He** crouched down behind a **massive** rock just as the dragon charged out of the cave, roaring. Albert peeked his head out, and to his horror the dragon was right in front of him **spewing** out a breath of fire.

Unexpectedly, the dragon remarked, "I am so sorry. I did not see you there."

Albert's mouth dropped wide open. Was he dreaming?

"Would you be so kind as to remove the thorns from my back? I was rolling around in the meadow, and they stuck to me."

Albert hesitated, but then agreed.

"Thank you kindly. Now, please hop on my back because I would like to take you for a ride and tell you my purpose here," requested the dragon.

Albert was now glad he had responded to the king's posters.

Because Albert was aware that he was a friendly dragon, Albert agreed. During the flight, the friendly dragon told him of his purpose. The dragon alighted from the ground and began to tell Albert his history.

"I come from a clan of evil dragons, who live a few days away from here in the depths of a vast, black forest. I believe in justice, but these dragons do not, so they banished me from the tribe. The day before I was banished, I overheard a horrifying plot to destroy all the kingdoms in the region."

"This is awful! We must warn the old king at once, so that he can notify the surrounding knights and their armies," Albert exclaimed.

"Please, show me the way," urged the dragon.

The king was on his balcony watching for Albert to return, when he noticed the dragon flying toward the castle.

"This is queer," the king thought. "I hired Albert to defeat the dragon, not take sides with him."

Hastily, the king **ascended** to the drawbridge. "What is the meaning of this?" the king demanded.

Albert replied, "This dragon is as harmless as a bunny. He has come to warn us of a clan of wicked dragons that are planning to attack the surrounding territories."   *dec.*

"How can we trust him?" the king asked.

"He has made no attempt to harm me or this kingdom. He is kind. We can trust him. I assure you," Albert insisted.   *dec.*

"Then I must notify the nearby kingdoms so we can join together and **pursue** them," the king declared.

After the neighboring kingdoms stuck together, they captured the nasty dragons with the help of brave Albert and the dragon of justice. Albert was **bestowed** with three bags of gold and remained friends with the dragon for the rest of his life, helping anyone in need.

Appendix 3: Student Samples

UNIT 6 SAMPLE

Lessons 19–20

Nathan E.

Lessons 19–20

6 January 2013

Note: I allow students who type papers to label sentence openers in brackets rather than in the left margin.

Juggernauts of the Middle Ages

Knights, <u>who</u> were the ironclad warriors of the Middle Ages, had many duties. First and foremost, a knight solemnly swore to protect his lord's life and land, in exchange for a part of the land the warrior safeguarded. Knights were like tanks. [2] In battle, they plowed through enemy foot soldiers on their horses and destroyed opposing forces. Eventually, they became the **elite** *dec.* class of warriors. <u>When</u> no conflict plagued the land, the **intrepid** knights had nothing to test their skills. So they **relished** the chance to compete with rival knights in a tournament to <u>hone</u> their battle skills. Since the government barely kept the country together, the **tenacious** warriors acted as policemen to keep law and order in the kingdom. Knights had many significant jobs.

Knights and their horses were known for the shining armor in which they were **clad**. [2] In the early days of the Middle Ages, armor was <u>forged</u> out of chain mail, <u>which</u> was ineffective at blocking axes and blades. But when the <u>lethal</u> crossbow was invented, new armor was <u>desperately</u> needed to protect the knights from the devastating bolts. So blacksmiths forged plates of metal to go over the chain mail. The plate armor became so complex that it took two men to buckle on the metal pieces. The armor was extremely costly. One suit made in Germany cost as much as a modern tank today. Unfortunately, <u>if</u> a knight stumbled and fell off his horse, then having to fight on foot in all that armor could be especially fatiguing. Knights were famous for the armor that both protected and hindered them.

The Crusades were a famous series of wars that many Christian knights and kings

Institute for Excellence in Writing

waged <u>because</u> they wanted to re-conquer the holy city of Jerusalem from the Muslims, <u>who</u>

were also known as Saracens. The Muslims were holding back rights for pilgrims to gain

access to the holy city. Passionately, Pope Urban II delivered a sermon, prompting knights

to conquer Jerusalem. The knights who responded to the call marched off to Jerusalem. The

Crusaders wore heavy armor, but the Saracens were quick and **<u>agile</u>**. But the **tenacious** Christian

fighters <u>eventually</u> captured the city. Then Saladin appeared. This Saracen leader thrashed the

crusading forces and retook Jerusalem. [2] During the third crusade, Richard the Lion Heart, the

formidable king of England conquered many cities and fortresses, but was ultimately **stymied** at

Jerusalem. The fourth crusade, a miserable failure, ended with the knights looting Constantinople

instead of liberating Jerusalem! Eventually the Saracens marched in, attacked, and held

Jerusalem for the rest of the Middle Ages. The Crusades are some of the most **renowned** wars

in history. Because of these wars and many like them, knights are well remembered as fearsome   *dec.*

fighters, armored juggernauts, and **tenacious** crusaders from the Middle Ages.

Appendix 3: Student Samples

UNIT 7 SAMPLE

Lesson 24

Arielle A.

Lesson 24

19 Mar. 2014

21st Century Magic

Dear Johnny,

Greetings from the 21st century <u>where</u> there is more magic than Merlin could ever dream. [3] Sadly, on the first day, I had just been dropped off in the 21st century when I realized I was falling. I was falling into a pond. Splash! It was a very strange pond with <u>smooth</u>, stone sides *dec.* and bottom. There were some steps leading out of the strange little pond, so I climbed them (they were not but two feet high all together). Once I reached the top, a wolf-like animal ran towards *dec.* me out of nowhere. I looked for something to defend myself but found nothing. The animal was closer now and barking <u>fiercely</u>. [2] At that moment, a young girl, <u>who</u> looked to be about 12, exited the house, and she called out, "Ashley, no!" The dog stopped its deep bark and <u>trotted</u> over to her, but it still eyed me suspiciously.

"Thank you," I stammered.

"Anything for a relative." The girl smiled and that's when I remembered Merlin mentioning someone would be expecting me here and that the story of my coming here had traveled through the generations.

"And you are…?" I asked.

"Arielle," the girl replied. "Please come in. Let me get you some water, you must be thirsty."

It was then that I realized I was parched. "Would you like me to retrieve some fresh water from the river?" I asked.

[4] Realizing I was not from her century, she smiled and then began to laugh. "We don't

need to get water that way anymore," she explained. "Come and I will show you." As we walked

into the house, I saw a **massive** metal box taller than I was, with handles on it.

"Here," she offered, **hastily** taking a cup made of paper. She pushed a lever, causing

rocks that I could see through to drop from a hole into the cup. Plop, plop, plop. Then she pushed   *3x*

another lever, and water flowed into the cup. She handed it to me.

After we had sat down, I inquired, "What is this?"

"That is ice and water," she explained. "The ice keeps the water cool."

"I guess I have a lot to learn," I stated with a smile.

"Don't worry, I am sure you will learn quickly," she replied. "It's only your first day here."

The next day Arielle informed me that we would be schooling today. Hoping to learn

many new things, I <u>groggily</u> pulled myself up and ate an odd breakfast soup called cereal. It was

like <u>crunchy</u>, sweet little bits of bread that were poured out of a box and into a bowl of milk. [3]

Shortly afterwards we began our day of schooling. Schooling involved a lesson from the Bible.

The family actually has their own copies of the Holy Book—three of them! Then there was a

history lesson, <u>which</u> came from a strange window they call a "TV." This subject I was forced

to skip—something about temporal anomalies and <u>ripping</u> apart the spacetime continuum. [2]

After history there was mathematics, which was taught via another new device called a computer.

Technology never ceases to amaze me. Following that was homework for a class called IEW, for   *dec.*

which I have also written a copy of this letter. I have learned this from my time here: <u>although</u>

inventions, places, and time have changed, GOD is constant. That is a great comfort. However,

I was most impressed by the technological advancements. I very much enjoyed their means of

transportation. Cars they are called. They are like fancy metal boxes with rubber wheels that move by themselves, much faster than any horse. I asked if I could take one with me, but they declined.

I will be returning to our time tomorrow, but I hope to visit here again someday as my time here was fascinating. The things in the 21st century might not be magic, but they are magical.

Sincerely,

Lyam

UNIT 9 SAMPLE

Lesson 26: "Genghis Khan and His Hawk" (with Advanced Lessons)

Tragedy Worth Remembering

"Genghis Khan and His Hawk" is a <u>classic</u> moral tale retold by Lori Verstegen and published by the Institute for Excellence in Writing in 2007. The story <u>centers</u> on one incident in the life of Genghis Khan, <u>who</u> ruled the vast Mongolian empire in the 1200s. [2]At the start of the story, the khan is on a hunting expedition with his beloved hawk. When he <u>accidentally</u> strays into a hot barren field, their time of pleasure turns **tragic**.

[4] Being set in a quiet forest in Mongolia, the story at first appears to be a happy one. As the title <u>implies</u>, there are two **dominant** characters: Genghis Khan and his hawk. The khan, <u>who</u> is a mighty warrior and a powerful ruler, cannot control his temper. This is his **tragic flaw**. The hawk is his loyal companion. [2] On every hunting trip, he eagerly accompanies his master and scouts for game. [3] Undoubtedly he loves the khan and is devoted to him.

The <u>conflict</u> begins when, after hunting in the hot sun all day, the khan needs some water to drink. <u>When he finally finds a trickle flowing from some rocks</u>, he is relieved. [3] Immediately he fills his cup and puts it to his mouth. But as soon as he does, his hawk dives down and <u>knocks</u> it from his hands. After yelling at his hawk, the khan refills his cup. Again the hawk spills it. The khan becomes **irate**. Finally, the third time this happens, the khan pulls out his sword and <u>angrily</u> strikes his friend dead

The climax happens when the khan finds the source of the water and discovers a dead, poisonous viper in the pool. Venom has contaminated the water. [2] At this <u>tragic</u> moment, the khan realizes that he has killed his best friend, who had only been trying to save his life. **Contritely** he **laments** his **rash** actions. The theme is obvious: Those who cannot control their tempers often see disaster.

Appendix 3: Student Samples

"Genghis Khan and His Hawk" is a **<u>compelling</u>** story that is both intriguing and **tragic** for many reasons. Because Verstegen does not reveal the viper until after the hawk is struck down, it is <u>bewildering</u> that the hawk keeps <u>knocking</u> the cup out of the khan's hands. It is sad when the king, <u>who</u> cannot control his temper, kills his loyal friend. [4] Adding to the emotion, the shock of the khan finding the viper in the water and the realization that the hawk has saved the khan's life causes more anger toward the khan. [3] Most <u>importantly</u>, though, the story has **valuable lessons** that will not easily be forgotten. [2] In the first place, friends should always be trusted. And, second, people should not act <u>hastily</u> <u>when</u> they are mad. It could be disastrous. Anyone who is angry should remember this **tragic story** before doing anything.

UNIT 9 THEME ANALYSIS SAMPLE

Lesson 27

The Power of Resolve

"The Determined Samurai" is a classic Japanese moral tale. This version was retold by Lori Verstegen and published by IEW in 2016. [2] For years it has been told to students of karate to inspire them to be passionate about their art.

The main character in this tale is a young samurai. The samurai were a noble warrior class in feudal Japan <u>where</u> the story takes place. [2] At the beginning of the story, the woman he loves is **tragically** killed by a <u>ruthless</u> tiger. This begins the conflict, <u>which</u> is that the samurai desires revenge. [4] **Anguishing** over the loss of his loved one, he hunts the **reprehensible** beast. [5] When he believes he has spotted it sleeping, he shoots his arrow. [6] It <u>pierces</u> the target. However, at the climax he discovers that he has shot a rock. [3] Evidently, the people of the village marvel at such **grandiose** strength and want him to repeat the feat. However, no matter how much he tries, he is unable to pierce the rock again. The story teaches that great things can only be accomplished by passion and determination.

The young samurai, like readers, learns that with **resolve** and passion there is power. He learns this because when he is <u>passionately</u> determined to kill the *truly terrible tiger*, he has enough strength to pierce a rock with an arrow. However, when he knows the rock is not the tiger, he cannot pierce it. He cannot fake the same passion nor shoot with the same **resolve** as before. Genuine desire is the key to success. This is true in many aspects of life. For example, when people are forced to do things they do not care about, little true effort is put in, and things are not done well. Even if they think they are trying to do their best, if there is no passion, something will be missing. On the other hand, when people want something enough, they find a way to succeed. A wise teacher will help his students become passionate about what they must learn, so they will succeed. That is why karate masters use this story of "The Determined Samurai." It is a story about understanding the power of **resolve**.

Appendix 3: Student Samples

UNIT 8 EXPANDED ESSAY

Lessons 28–30

Geneva S.

Lessons 28–30

13 May 2015

Great Men of the Renaissance

Who were the great painters of the Renaissance? Who were the scientists of this time who changed people's perspective? [6] What was the Renaissance? The Renaissance followed the Middle Ages, around 1300, and then spread through Europe. [2] In French, the name "renaissance" means "rebirth," in this case referring to the Greek and Roman culture and love of learning. Artists like Leonardo da Vinci and Michelangelo cleverly developed new techniques to paint, and scientists like Copernicus and Galileo, who questioned traditional ideas about the universe, pursued new and incredible discoveries, changing people's perspectives on many different things. Truly the Renaissance was a time of great thinkers.

Born in 1452, Leonardo da Vinci is known as "the Ultimate Renaissance Man." Among his many talents, he was a renowned painter. [5] When he was fourteen, Leonardo traveled to Florence, Italy, to learn painting from Andrea Del Verrocchio. [3] Shortly after, Verrocchio asked da Vinci to paint an angel. When he saw the boy's skill, "he put down his brush and swore never to paint again" (M. in Verstegen 194). Leonardo had an immense interest in painting as realistically as possible, so he studied people in order to understand their proportions perfectly. He then painted a famous painting, *The Lord's Supper*, on the wall of a church. [5] As da Vinci did not like the paint he was given, he chose to make his own. This was a tedious project. *The Lord's Supper* is sadly often in need of repair, as the paint flakes. This masterpiece, which took three years to complete, is one of the most reproduced pieces of art in the world. In 1499, da

Vinci returned to Florence and painted the *Mona Lisa*. [2] Before this time, all portraits had been painted from the neck up, making them look as though people's heads were floating in the air. But Leonardo also painted Mona Lisa's hands, giving her a more realistic look. In 1517, Leonardo moved to France. Regrettably, this great Renaissance artist died two years later.

Born in 1575, Michelangelo is <u>revered</u> as one of the greatest artists of all time. Because of its realism, his work is widely admired. He created <u>incredible</u> sculptures including *David*, the *Madonna*, and the *Pieta*, a statue of Mary with Jesus after his death. His last figure, which was of Moses, was made for the tomb of a pope. [6] He also loved to paint. Imitating da Vinci's love of realistic portraits, he spent two years on his back working on the ceiling of the Sistine chapel. [2] After this achievement, Michelangelo became known as "Il Divino" (the Divine). [5] Although he lived a long life, he <u>eventually</u> died in 1564 at age 88. [3] Undoubtedly, his amazing use of color and the three-dimensional appearance of his work will be remembered forever.

The Renaissance was not just a time of great painters, but also of many scientific discoveries. Nicolaus Copernicus is remembered as the first great astronomer. Born in 1473, Copernicus was rich and very smart. [3] Tragically, by the time he was ten, both his parents were dead and he had been sent to live with his uncle. He attended the University of Cracow <u>where</u> he was taught mathematics and painting. [2] By the time he graduated, he had developed an <u>immense</u> interest in space. Most people in that time believed in a geocentric, earth-centered universe, whereas Copernicus was firmly convinced the sun was the center of our solar system. [6] This is correct. [5] After he came to this conclusion, he wrote a book, called *De Revolutionibus Orbium Coelestum*, <u>which</u> was eventually banned by the Roman Catholic Church. Protestant theologians also disregarded his work, calling him a "fool." [3] Sadly, Nicolaus died in 1543, and it was not until many years later after his book had been widely read that he became famous as an astronomer. Copernicus is one of the most **renowned** astronomers of all time.

Galileo Galilei is often called the father of the scientific method. Born in Pisa, Italy, this great man was <u>intrigued</u> by our universe and made many discoveries. [5] Because he was curious, he conducted many experiments, including dropping different sized objects off the Leaning Tower of Pisa to prove that size does not change the time something takes to reach the ground. [2] After this, he worked <u>steadily</u> to improve the telescope, improving the magnification from three to twenty. This was helpful to him, <u>as</u> he then started to stargaze. [3] Impressively, he confirmed that the sun is the center of the solar system. [2] Until then, many people still believed that the earth was in the center and the sun rotated around the earth. [6] Galileo convinced many otherwise. He wrote several books including *Dialogue Concerning the Two Chief World Systems* and *Discourse on Bodies in Water*. He was an <u>incredible</u> man who helped our world in more ways than one. He was Galileo, father of science.

A new age, the Renaissance, was brought on by great men. [2] In this era, artists like da Vinci and Michelangelo **stunned** everyone with new and <u>magnificent</u> art, and scientists like Copernicus and Galileo <u>exploded</u> with new ideas and advances. [5]Although the painters and scientists alike <u>successfully</u> changed the world in their day, their greatest achievement is that they have continued to inspire people to keep learning and make new discoveries today. [6] Their memories live on. [5] As our world progresses, these great Renaissance men still inspire us to look for what others cannot see.

———————————————

Bibliography

Combee, Jerry. "*Michelangelo.*" Class handout.

"Nicolaus Copernicus." *Bio.com*. A&E Networks Television, n.d. Web. 12 May 2015.

Verstegen, Lori. *Medieval History-Based Writing Lessons*. Locust Grove: Institute for Excellence

in Writing, 2015. 193–204. Print.

VOCABULARY STORY SAMPLE

Lesson 31

Students are encouraged to use vocabulary words from previous classes, too, so this story has many words from the US History-Based Lessons in addition to those from these Medieval History-Based Lessons.

Chloe P.

Lesson 31

8 May 2014

The Little Red Hen

Once upon a time there was a **secluded**, **serene** farm filled with **indolent** animals, that is, except for the little red hen. On an **impeccable** sunny spring day, just right for starting a new crop of wheat, the little red hen **encountered** a **myriad** wheat seeds that the **hasty** farmer had dropped. The little red hen **apprehended** the seeds and exclaimed, "I will plant them and soon have bread! Who will help plant the seeds?" she asked.

"Not I," **rashly** replied the **obstinate** dog.

"Not I," **scorned** the **smug**, **capricious** cat.

"Not I," **scowled** the **perturbed** pig.

The little red hen would not be **stymied** by the **indolent** animals, so she found a **vacant** lot and began **toiling** away with her chicks, planting seeds here and there. After some long days of **interminable** weeding, watering, and tending, the wheat was ready to be cut and taken to the mill.

"Who will help me chop down the wheat and take it to the mill," the little red hen asked.

"Not I," **rashly** replied the **obstinate** dog.

"Not I," **scorned** the **smug**, **capricious** cat.

"Not I," **scowled** the **perturbed** pig.

The little red hen **contemplated** her choices: should she give up or should she **pursue** her dream and start **toiling** away again? The little red hen **confronted** the wheat patch and **tenaciously** continued her work with her helpful chicks because she saw **potential** in the wheat. **Fatigued** from their **perseverance**, the little red hen and her chicks hauled the **massive** stalks of wheat to the mill. The little red hen knew it would be ground into flour **imminently**, so she stayed until it was done.

When they returned home with the flour, the hen's dreams plummeted when one of her chicks asked, "How can we get this flour into the kitchen, so we can bake our bread?"

But to her relief, the door opened. So, the little red hen asked, "Who will help me bake the bread?"

"Not I," **rashly** replied the **obstinate** dog.

"Not I," **scorned** the **smug**, **capricious** cat.

"Not I," **scowled** the **perturbed** pig.

So, she and her chicks **resolved** to do it themselves. After the long, **tedious** work was done, and the **din** in the kitchen was over, the little red hen and her chicks were **elated** as they looked down at their loaf of bread, **embellished** with seeds and nuts from the pantry. The little red hen **extolled** the **incredible** work her chicks had done.

"Now let's go outside to **relish** and eat our **impeccable** bread," the little red hen declared.

The dog, cat, and pig were **stunned** to see the loaf of bread and hurried to the shady spot where the family of poultry were about to eat, after **devoutly** giving thanks to God. When the animals approached, the little red hen could not help but laugh at the **ludicrous**, **abashed** looks on their faces.

"We have **reformed** from our **indolent** ways and would like to help you eat your bread," explained the animals **gravely**.

"No!" **rebuked** the **intrepid** little red hen. "You **squandered** your time when you could have helped me. Now my chicks and I will enjoy the fruit of our labor."

Feeling more **provoked** than **contrite**, the **indignant** animals **spewed** back, "Fine! We do not want your **repugnant**, **fetid** bread anyway!"

With that the **insolent** dog, cat, and pig stormed off, leaving the little red hen and her chicks to their delicious bread. And that is the story of the **renowned** little red hen!

Appendix 4: Adding Literature

Great literature will be a valuable addition to these lessons. There are many, many great books set in medieval times. The books below are suggested because their stories provide background to the compositions students will write in these lessons. Some are easy enough for all students to read on their own, but others may be better read aloud. Reading aloud has many benefits and should be part of any quality education. Audiobooks are also a wonderful option. Students can follow along in the actual book.

The classic tales about Beowulf, 1001 Arabian Nights, King Arthur, and Robin Hood can be found in many different versions. For elementary classes, search for quality children's versions of these. I have listed the versions my 5th–8th grade classes use.

Lessons	Book
3–6	***Beowulf* by Michael Morpurgo** This is a simplified, illustrated children's version that tells the basic story of the classic epic poem. The original work is famous because it is possibly the oldest surviving epic poem written in the language of the Anglo-Saxons. It was written in England around the sixth or seventh century but is set in Scandinavia before the Angles and Saxons migrated to Britain. The story is fiction, but some people and events in the story are historical. It helps us understand the Anglo-Saxon culture of warriors who fought loyally for their kings according to their code of honor.
7–8	Selected tales from ***1001 Arabian Nights* by Geraldine McCaughrean** or a younger children's version: ***Arabian Nights*** from the Classic Starts series (Sterling Publishing Co) ISBN 978-1-4027-4573-7 The background of these many short stories set in Arabia is that the king has decided that each night he must kill his wife (so she does not have time to stop loving him). Each day he takes a new bride. So brave Shahrazad devises a clever plan to spare her life and stop the killings. Each night she tells him a story that keeps the king wanting to hear more. In these books kids will meet such famous characters as Sinbad the Sailor and Ali Baba. Read all the stories or choose a few.
9–13	***The Legend of King Arthur* by Roger Lancelyn Green** (selected chapters) or a children's version Green's telling of the most famous legend of medieval times begins with the story of the sword in the stone and includes all of the legendary people and places the story is famous for: Merlin, Excalibur, Camelot, the knights of the Round Table, and more. However, be warned that there is much bloodshed and magic throughout the story. Since each chapter is its own story, it is possible to pick and choose chapters to familiarize your students with the legends rather than reading the entire book.

14–17	***The King's Shadow* by Elizabeth Alder**
	Don't skip this wonderful, action-packed story filled with history! It is the story of a mute Welsh serf named Evyn. He is sold to be the slave of the common-law wife of Harold Godwinson. Evyn travels with Harold on a military expedition as a scout, and the two develop a father-son-like relationship. When Godwinson becomes the king of England, Evyn is made his squire. He stands by the king's side at the Battle of Hastings and lives to write Harold's life story.
18–19	***Otto of the Silver Hand* by Howard Pyle**
	This is the story of a young boy named Otto who is the son of a robber baron in medieval Germany. After the death of his mother, he is brought to a monastery as a baby but eventually is retrieved by his father and exposed to the harsh world of feuding households. Through Otto's perspective of both worlds, he learns to forgive, and he gains much wisdom. He becomes one of the king's most trusted advisors.
20–23	***Robin Hood* by J. Walker McSpadden** or a children's version
	The legend begins with the transformation of young noble Robert Fitzooth into Robin Hood. He leads a band of "merry men" in robbing the rich to give to the poor when England is suffering under the rule of King Henry II and then greedy Prince John while King Richard is off fighting the Third Crusade.
23	***Marco Polo* by Demi**
	This is a 64-page picture book that can be read in a day or two. It is filled with beautiful pictures and fascinating information about medieval Europe, the Middle East, and China.
24–27	***The Kite Rider* by Geraldine McCaughrean**
	This story is set in thirteenth-century China when Kublai Khan is ruling. It is the story of a poor peasant boy who is given the chance to escape poverty by becoming a kite rider in a circus. Not only does he earn money, he earns freedom and unexpected fame. The story is a window into China's medieval culture and superstitions.
28–31	***Crispin: The Cross of Lead* by Avi**
	This is a Newberry Award winning story set in fourteenth-century England. *Book Report* says it "is a superb combination of mystery, historical fiction, and a coming-of-age tale … Breathlessly paced, beautifully written, and filled with details of life in the Middle Ages."

These sheets are recommended for junior high students. If you would like students to use them when they read, instruct them to make copies of this master. They will need pages 255–256 each week they read. They will page 257 for each book they complete.

Weekly Literature Response Sheet

Name: _____   Date: _____

Book Title: _____   Chapter(s): _____

Vocabulary

From the chapter(s) you read, find three unfamiliar words or three quality words that you might like to use in your own writing. In the chart below, write each word, its definition, and the sentence you found it in.

1.	definition
sentence	

2.	definition
sentence	

3.	definition
sentence	

Dress-Ups

From the chapter(s), write two sentences that contain dress-ups you like. Look for the ones you have learned thus far. Underline each dress-up.

1. _____

   _____

2. _____

   _____

Decorations or Imagery

From the chapter(s), write a passage that contains a good five-senses description, a triple extension, or a decoration you have learned thus far, such as alliteration, simile, or 3sss. You may also include any other literary element of style you may know, such as personification or onomatopoeia (extra credit if you write more than one).

_____

_____

_____

Journal

Pretend you are a character in the story. Briefly tell the most important events in the chapter(s) from your point of view. Include your thoughts and feelings.

I am _____

_____

_____

_____

Final Literature Response Sheet

After you finish a book, use your own paper to answer the following questions:

1. What is the title and author of the book?

2. What is the setting of the book? Describe it.

3. Describe each main character. (no more than four)

4. What is the main conflict of the story? (What is the main problem, want, or need of the main character?) Write in complete sentences, but be brief.

5. What is the climax? (What event leads to the conflict being solved?)

6. What is the resolution? (How do things work out in the end?)

7. What themes are present in the story? How? (A theme is a truth that can be applied to all times, a virtue that is upheld, or an evil that is condemned. Some common themes are courage, loyalty, redemption, faith, the power of love, good triumphs over evil, perseverance, the value of family, the evils of greed, prejudice, lust for power.)

8. What is your favorite part of the story? Why?

9. What other things do you like or not like?

Appendix 4: Adding Literature

Appendix 5: Vocabulary

There is a sheet of four vocabulary cards for most of the lessons. In lessons that have cards, you will be instructed to cut them out and place them in a plastic bag or pencil pouch for easy reference. Each week you should study the words for the current lesson and continue to review words from previous lessons. You should try to use the vocabulary words in your compositions. For this purpose, you may use any of the words, even from lessons you have not yet had if you would like to look ahead.

Many students enjoy the challenge of using as many of the words as they can, especially if the teacher offers some type of reward for doing so. I give one or two tickets for each vocabulary word used. See Appendix 6 for an explanation of tickets.

For convenience, the following chart shows the words that go with each lesson and where quizzes fall. Quizzes are cumulative and cover all the words listed above them.

Quizzes follow the chart. Teachers who do not want students to see the quizzes ahead of time may ask you to tear them from your books and turn them in at the beginning of the school year. This is at the discretion of your teacher.

Answer keys are on the back of each quiz.

Vocabulary Cards

The cards are only in the Student Book. When reviewing or playing games with words, teachers should borrow cards from a student or use the chart on the following pages.

Vocabulary at a Glance

Lesson 1	fetid	stinky
	massive	huge
	dilapidated	partly ruined; broken down
	intrepid	fearless
Lesson 2	stunned	shocked
	flee	to run away, as from danger
	desecrate	to destroy the beauty or holiness of a sacred place
	tenacious	determined; not giving up
Lesson 3	melancholy	gloomy; causing sadness
	imminent	happening soon
	bewildered	puzzled
	embellish	to decorate; to make more interesting by adding fanciful details
Lesson 4	resolved	firmly determined to do something
	brandish	to wave threateningly
	spew	to gush out, especially in anger or disgust
	fatal	causing death or ruin
Lesson 5 Quiz 1	no new words	
Lesson 6	extol	to praise highly
	fatigued	tired or worn out
	rebuke	to blame or find fault with
	intrigued	curious or fascinated by something
Lesson 7	pursue	to chase
	hastily	quickly and with little thought
	vacant	empty
	credible	believable
Lesson 8	anguish	great pain or suffering in mind or body
	insolent	boldly rude or insulting; disrespectful
	restrain	to hold back from doing something
	gravely	seriously; solemnly
Lesson 9	disclosed	uncovered or revealed
	contrite	sincerely sorry
	scowl	to look angry
	dislodge	to remove; to force out
Lesson 10 Quiz 2	no new words	
Lesson 11	prominent	standing out; leading, important, or well-known
	myriad	a great number
	virtue	a moral or admirable quality
	endure	to continue to exist; to hold out against something

Lesson 12	uniform	
	perturbed	
	foremost	
	reform	an improvement (noun); to form again (verb)
Lesson 13	bestow	to give or grant
	devout	devoted to religion
	renowned	famous; of good reputation
	proficient	skilled or expert
Lesson 14 Quiz 3	no new words	
Lesson 15	apprehend	to seize
	stymied	blocked
	plummet	to drop straight down
	interminable	seemingly endless
Lesson 16	relish	to like very much
	abashed	embarrassed or ashamed
	ludicrous	ridiculous
	capriciously	acting without apparent reason or cause
Lesson 17 Quiz 4	din	a loud, confused, or clanging noise
	crane	to stretch out one's neck
	reprehensible	deserving blame
	repugnant	distasteful; repulsive
Lesson 18	grandiose	grand in an impressive way
	serene	calm and peaceful
	toil	to work hard; to labor
	contrive	to scheme
Lesson 19	feeble	weak
	clad	clothed
	scorn	reject with disgust
	elite	a socially superior group
Lesson 20	agile	able to move quickly and easily
	impeccable	perfect
	smug	highly pleased with oneself
	indolent	lazy
Lesson 21–25 Quiz 5	no new words	
Lesson 26	analyze	to examine the parts of something
	aghast	showing signs of horror
	tragic	extremely unfortunate
	rash	too hasty in action; reckless
Lesson 27 Final Test		

Appendix 5: Vocabulary

Vocabulary Quiz 1

brandish	fatal	intrepid	resolved
desecrate	fetid	massive	spew
embellish	imminent	melancholy	stunned

Fill in the blanks with the appropriate word. Be sure to spell correctly.

1. stinky   1. _____

2. huge   2. _____

3. fearless   3. _____

4. shocked   4. _____

5. to destroy the holiness of a sacred place   5. _____

6. to gush out in anger or disgust   6. _____

7. gloomy; causing sadness   7. _____

8. happening soon   8. _____

9. to decorate   9. _____

10. firmly determined to do something   10. _____

11. to wave threateningly   11. _____

12. causing death or ruin   12. _____

Appendix 5: Vocabulary

Vocabulary Quiz 1 Answer Key

brandish	fatal	intrepid	resolved
desecrate	fetid	massive	spew
embellish	imminent	melancholy	stunned

Fill in the blanks with the appropriate word. Be sure to spell correctly.

1. stinky

2. huge

3. fearless

4. shocked

5. to destroy the holiness of a sacred place

6. to gush out in anger or disgust

7. gloomy; causing sadness

8. happening soon

9. to decorate

10. firmly determined to do something

11. to wave threateningly

12. causing death or ruin

1. ___*fetid*___

2. ___*massive*___

3. ___*intrepid*___

4. ___*stunned*___

5. ___*desecrate*___

6. ___*spew*___

7. ___*melancholy*___

8. ___*imminent*___

9. ___*embellish*___

10. ___*resolved*___

11. ___*brandish*___

12. ___*fatal*___

Institute for Excellence in Writing

Vocabulary Quiz 2

anguish	dilapidated	hastily	scowl
bewildered	extol	insolent	spew
contrite	flee	rebuke	tenacious
credible	gravely	restrain	

Fill in the blanks with the appropriate word. Be sure to spell correctly.

1. partly ruined; broken down

1. _____

2. to run away, as from danger

2. _____

3. determined; not giving up

3. _____

4. puzzled

4. _____

5. to gush out, especially in anger or disgust

5. _____

6. to praise highly

6. _____

7. to blame or find fault with

7. _____

8. quickly and with little thought

8. _____

9. believable

9. _____

10. great pain or suffering in mind or body

10. _____

11. boldly rude or insulting; disrespectful

11. _____

12. to hold back from doing something

12. _____

13. seriously; solemnly

13. _____

14. sincerely sorry

14. _____

15. to look angry

15. _____

Vocabulary Quiz 2   Answer Key

anguish	dilapidated	hastily	scowl
bewildered	extol	insolent	spew
contrite	flee	rebuke	tenacious
credible	gravely	restrain	

Fill in the blanks with the appropriate word. Be sure to spell correctly.

1. partly ruined; broken down

2. to run away, as from danger

3. determined; not giving up

4. puzzled

5. to gush out, especially in anger or disgust

6. to praise highly

7. to blame or find fault with

8. quickly and with little thought

9. believable

10. great pain or suffering in mind or body

11. boldly rude or insulting; disrespectful

12. to hold back from doing something

13. seriously; solemnly

14. sincerely sorry

15. to look angry

1. *dilapidated*

2. *flee*

3. *tenacious*

4. *bewildered*

5. *spew*

6. *extol*

7. *rebuke*

8. *hastily*

9. *credible*

10. *anguish*

11. *insolent*

12. *restrain*

13. *gravely*

14. *contrite*

15. *scowl*

Institute for Excellence in Writing

Vocabulary Quiz 3

bestow	endure	perturbed	renowned
devout	foremost	proficient	uniform
disclosed	intrigued	pursue	vacant
dislodge	myriad	reform	

Fill in the blanks with the appropriate word. Be sure to spell correctly.

1. curious or fascinated by something   1. _____

2. empty   2. _____

3. uncovered or revealed   3. _____

4. to chase   4. _____

5. to remove; to force out   5. _____

6. a great number   6. _____

7. to continue to exist; to hold out   7. _____

8. of the same form or manner as others   8. _____

9. annoyed   9. _____

10. first in time, place, or order   10. _____

11. an improvement; to make better   11. _____

12. to give or grant   12. _____

13. devoted to religion   13. _____

14. famous; of good reputation   14. _____

15. skilled or expert   15. _____

Vocabulary Quiz 3 Answer Key

bestow	endure	perturbed	renowned
devout	foremost	proficient	uniform
disclosed	intrigued	pursue	vacant
dislodge	myriad	reform	

Fill in the blanks with the appropriate word. Be sure to spell correctly.

1. curious or fascinated by something
2. empty
3. uncovered or revealed
4. to chase
5. to remove; to force out
6. a great number
7. to continue to exist; to hold out
8. of the same form or manner as others
9. annoyed
10. first in time, place, or order
11. an improvement; to make better
12. to give or grant
13. devoted to religion
14. famous; of good reputation
15. skilled or expert

1. *intrigued*
2. *vacant*
3. *disclosed*
4. *pursue*
5. *dislodge*
6. *myriad*
7. *endure*
8. *uniform*
9. *perturbed*
10. *foremost*
11. *reform*
12. *bestow*
13. *devout*
14. *renowned*
15. *proficient*

Institute for Excellence in Writing

Vocabulary Quiz 4

abashed	dislodge	interminable	relish
apprehend	fatigued	ludicrous	stymied
capriciously	gravely	plummet	virtue
credible	insolent	prominent	

Fill in the blanks with the appropriate word. Be sure to spell correctly.

1. tired or worn out

2. believable

3. boldly rude or insulting; disrespectful

4. seriously; solemnly

5. to remove; to force out

6. standing out; leading

7. a moral or admirable quality

8. to like very much

9. to seize

10. blocked

11. to drop straight down

12. seemingly endless

13. acting without reason or cause

14. ridiculous

15. embarrassed or ashamed

1. _____

2. _____

3. _____

4. _____

5. _____

6. _____

7. _____

8. _____

9. _____

10. _____

11. _____

12. _____

13. _____

14. _____

15. _____

Vocabulary Quiz 4   Answer Key

abashed	dislodge	interminable	relish
apprehend	fatigued	ludicrous	stymied
capriciously	gravely	plummet	virtue
credible	insolent	prominent	

Fill in the blanks with the appropriate word. Be sure to spell correctly.

1. tired or worn out

2. believable

3. boldly rude or insulting; disrespectful

4. seriously; solemnly

5. to remove; to force out

6. standing out; leading

7. a moral or admirable quality

8. to like very much

9. to seize

10. blocked

11. to drop straight down

12. seemingly endless

13. acting without reason or cause

14. ridiculous

15. embarrassed or ashamed

1. _fatigued_

2. _credible_

3. _insolent_

4. _gravely_

5. _dislodge_

6. _prominent_

7. _virtue_

8. _relish_

9. _apprehend_

10. _stymied_

11. _plummet_

12. _interminable_

13. _capriciously_

14. _ludicrous_

15. _abashed_

Vocabulary Quiz 5

agile	grandiose	proficient	smug
din	indolent	reform	stymied
extol	intrepid	reprehensible	toil
feeble	ludicrous	scorn	

Fill in the blanks with the appropriate word. Be sure to spell correctly.

1. fearless   1. _____

2. to praise highly   2. _____

3. an improvement; to make better   3. _____

4. skilled or expert   4. _____

5. blocked   5. _____

6. ridiculous   6. _____

7. a loud, confused, or clanging noise   7. _____

8. deserving blame   8. _____

9. grand in an impressive way   9. _____

10. to work hard; to labor   10. _____

11. weak   11. _____

12. reject with disgust   12. _____

13. able to move quickly or easily   13. _____

14. highly pleased with oneself   14. _____

15. lazy   15. _____

Vocabulary Quiz 5   Answer Key

agile	grandiose	proficient	smug
din	indolent	reform	stymied
extol	intrepid	reprehensible	toil
feeble	ludicrous	scorn	

Fill in the blanks with the appropriate word. Be sure to spell correctly.

1. fearless

2. to praise highly

3. an improvement; to make better

4. skilled or expert

5. blocked

6. ridiculous

7. a loud, confused, or clanging noise

8. deserving blame

9. grand in an impressive way

10. to work hard; to labor

11. weak

12. reject with disgust

13. able to move quickly or easily

14. highly pleased with oneself

15. lazy

1. *intrepid*

2. *extol*

3. *reform*

4. *proficient*

5. *stymied*

6. *ludicrous*

7. *din*

8. *reprehensible*

9. *grandiose*

10. *toil*

11. *feeble*

12. *scorn*

13. *agile*

14. *smug*

15. *indolent*

Final Vocabulary Quiz

abashed	contrite	fatal	interminable	restrain
aghast	contrive	feeble	intrigued	serene
analyze	crane	imminent	rash	tenacious
anguish	elite	impeccable	renowned	tragic
brandish	embellish	indolent	repugnant	vacant

Fill in the blanks with the appropriate word. Be sure to spell correctly.

1. to examine the parts of something
2. lazy
3. perfect
4. to scheme
5. too hasty in action
6. calm and peaceful
7. determined; not giving up
8. happening soon
9. to hold back from doing something
10. extremely unfortunate
11. showing signs of horror
12. a socially superior group
13. weak
14. distasteful; repulsive
15. to stretch out one's neck
16. embarrassed or ashamed
17. seemingly endless
18. famous; of good reputation
19. sincerely sorry
20. great pain or suffering in mind or body
21. empty
22. curious or fascinated by something
23. causing death or ruin
24. to wave threateningly
25. to decorate

1. _____
2. _____
3. _____
4. _____
5. _____
6. _____
7. _____
8. _____
9. _____
10. _____
11. _____
12. _____
13. _____
14. _____
15. _____
16. _____
17. _____
18. _____
19. _____
20. _____
21. _____
22. _____
23. _____
24. _____
25. _____

Final Vocabulary Quiz   Answer Key

abashed	contrite	fatal	interminable	restrain
aghast	contrive	feeble	intrigued	serene
analyze	crane	imminent	rash	tenacious
anguish	elite	impeccable	renowned	tragic
brandish	embellish	indolent	repugnant	vacant

Fill in the blanks with the appropriate word. Be sure to spell correctly.

1. to examine the parts of something
2. lazy
3. perfect
4. to scheme
5. too hasty in action
6. calm and peaceful
7. determined; not giving up
8. happening soon
9. to hold back from doing something
10. extremely unfortunate
11. showing signs of horror
12. a socially superior group
13. weak
14. distasteful; repulsive
15. to stretch out one's neck
16. embarrassed or ashamed
17. seemingly endless
18. famous; of good reputation
19. sincerely sorry
20. great pain or suffering in mind or body
21. empty
22. curious or fascinated by something
23. causing death or ruin
24. to wave threateningly
25. to decorate

1. _analyze_
2. _indolent_
3. _impeccable_
4. _contrive_
5. _rash_
6. _serene_
7. _tenacious_
8. _imminent_
9. _restrain_
10. _tragic_
11. _aghast_
12. _elite_
13. _feeble_
14. _repugnant_
15. _crane_
16. _abashed_
17. _interminable_
18. _renowned_
19. _contrite_
20. _anguish_
21. _vacant_
22. _intrigued_
23. _fatal_
24. _brandish_
25. _embellish_

Institute for Excellence in Writing

Appendix 6: Motivating Students: Tickets and Games

Students should be rewarded for jobs well done. Positive reinforcement is a wonderful motivator. In my classes, I have found a ticket system to be extremely effective. To use such a system, purchase a roll of raffle tickets from an office supply store. In addition, I make 5-, 10-, and 25-point tickets printed on colored paper. (A 2 columns x 5 rows table works well.)

Give tickets for any of the advanced lessons done and for anything done particularly well. I always give a ticket for each vocabulary word used. I also give three tickets for each decoration used.

Periodically I have contests for tickets, such as "Best Title" or the best of each type of decoration. I also give tickets for winning review games such as those described below. Tickets may be used in an auction twice a year: once just before Christmas and once at the end of the year.

The Auction

There are many ways to do an auction. Here is how I do mine. You will want a calculator.

1. Students bring items to auction to class. These can be new or they can be items they have at home and think someone else would like. I sometimes fill in with items from a dollar store and with candy. Two items per student works well.

2. Students put their tickets in an envelope with their name and number of tickets written on the outside and turn them in to you.

3. Write the students' names and number of tickets on the whiteboard in order from greatest to least. Instead of having students physically hand you tickets when they buy and sell things, you can subtract and add from their totals.

4. To begin, ask the student with the most tickets which item he would like to have auctioned first. When he chooses, he is bidding, so he should choose something he would like. Bids must begin at 25 or higher.

5. Students who would like the item continue to bid. Highest bidder gets the item. His bid is subtracted from his ticket total and added to the total of the person who brought that item (maximum of 100 is added).

6. Repeat this process, letting the student listed second on the board choose next. However, students who have bought an item may not bid on another until everyone has one. (This means the last person will get what he wants of what is left for the minimum bid of 25.)

7. Once everyone has one item, it is open bidding for what is left.

Games

The best motivator I have found in all my years of teaching is playing games that teach and review concepts. Below are a few that are suggested in the lessons. If you love games as much as I do, *Teaching with Games* (published by IEW) has many more ideas for games adaptable for any subject, any grade level, and any number of players.

No-Noose Hangman

1. Think of anything you would like to review. Put it into a simple list or phrase. For example, if you want to remind your students to highlight the key words in their topic sentence and clincher, you might use "highlight key words" as your phrase.

2. On a whiteboard, write a blank for each letter in your phrase:

   — — — — — — — — —

   — — —   — — — — —

3. Students take turns guessing letters, one letter per turn. If the letter is in the puzzle, place it on the correct blank(s) and give the student a ticket for each time it is used. (Exception: Do not give tickets for vowels.) If the letter is not in the puzzle, write it on the bottom of the whiteboard, so no one else will guess it.

4. Anytime a student knows the phrase, he may raise his hand to solve the puzzle. *It does not have to be his turn.*

5. If he solves the puzzle correctly, he receives 3 tickets. If he can then answer a bonus question about the phrase, he receives 2 more. (A bonus question for the above puzzle could be, "In which sentences do you highlight the key words?")

6. Repeat with several puzzles.

Vocabulary Hangman

To play with vocabulary words, use the definition as the puzzle. When solved, the student or team who solved it must give you the matching word to receive the points.

Vocabulary Elimination or Around the World

1. Divide the class into groups of three or four students. Try to have an even number of groups. Go to one group. Read a definition of a vocabulary word. The first student in that group to shout out the matching word gets a ticket. Continue with the first group until one student has three tickets. He has eliminated the rest of his group. Repeat with the other groups.

2. Repeat with half of the winners as one group, then with the other half. Finally, repeat with the two remaining students. The winner of that round receives five extra tickets.

Around the World is similar. Start with two students. Read a definition. The first to shout the correct vocabulary word receives a ticket and moves on to challenge the next student. Continue in the same way. The winner always moves on to the next student. If one student makes it all the way "around the world" (beats everyone in the class), he gets five extra tickets.

Vocabulary Lightning

To prepare: You will need a stack of vocabulary cards (borrow from a student), a whiteboard (optional), and a timer.

To play, divide the class into two or three teams. Then, for each round, do the following:

1. Choose one or two players from one of the teams to come up in front of their team. Show them the stack of vocabulary cards with the word sides up. (They may not look at the definition side.)

2. Their job will be to try to get their team to say as many of the vocabulary words as they can in one minute. To do so, once the timer is set, they look at the first word and give their team clues, such as saying the definition, acting out the word, or describing or drawing the picture on the card. They may not say things such as what letter the word begins with or what it rhymes with. (Optional: Do not allow talking—only acting or drawing.)

3. As soon as someone from their team shouts the correct word, you (the teacher) should place the card on a table and move to the next word. If they get stuck on a word they may "pass" it after counting to five (the penalty for a pass). Be sure to place passed word cards in a separate stack from the word cards they guess correctly.

4. When the time is up, count the number of words their team guessed. Then, let the other team(s) have a turn in the same way. The team who guesses the most words wins that round. Play several rounds if you have time.

Vocabulary Pictionary

Need:
*Two whiteboards (or one large one with a line sectioning it) or substitute paper and pencils
*Two whiteboard markers
*a die (optional)

1. Divide the class into two teams. Assign each a whiteboard. Call one person from each team to the front of the class. Have them each roll the die to determine the number of points their team will receive if they win the round. Instruct them to write that number on the top of the whiteboard, so it is not forgotten. (The die is optional. You can just make each round won worth a point.)

2. Show the two students who came up which vocabulary word you want them to draw. (They will both draw the same word.)

3. When you say, "Go," they must draw a picture to try to get their team to say the chosen word. They may not include any letters or numbers in their drawings. The first team to guess the word receives the number of points rolled on their die if they can tell you the definition of the word. (Subtract 2 pts if they cannot.) The other team erases the points they rolled. Play again with two new drawers.

The Five-Senses Game
To prepare, write the following on the whiteboard:

Looks   Sounds   Feels   Smells/Tastes

Divide the class into two or three teams. One person from each team comes to the front of his team. Tell each of them the same word from below (or make up your own that might be in their story or essay). Tell everyone the category of the word.

Food/Drink: popcorn, Coke, pizza, hot dog ...
Objects Outside: skyscraper, bus, train, helicopter, lawn mower ...
Inside: refrigerator, lamp, canned food, ...

The students at the front must take turns giving a five-senses word about the object. After each of the clues, the team of the student who gave it tries to guess the word. (Teacher writes the clue under the matching sense for all to see and remember.) For example, if the word is *kitten*, the student from Team A must give one five-senses word as a clue (e.g., *furry*). Then his team tries to guess the word. If wrong, the student from Team B then gives a one-word clue (e.g., *meow*), and his team guesses. Continue until a team guesses the word. That team gets a point.

Repeat with two new students and a new word. Be sure students understand that they may only say one word and that it must be a word that appeals to one of the five senses.

Sentence Stretching

On sixteen note cards write one of each of the following. (Each element of style will be on two different cards.) Omit ones you have not yet taught.

who-which clause	www.asia clause	quality adj	strong verb (replace the verb given in the sentence)
alliteration	simile	-ly adverb	3sss

To play

1. Divide the class into teams of two to four students.

2. One at a time, each team chooses three cards.

3. Each group has two minutes to stretch the basic sentence you put on the whiteboard by adding the three elements they chose. They may add more detail to the sentence in order to accomplish this. (Teachers, you may use a basic sentence from those suggested below or make up your own.)

All teams should be encouraged to add vocabulary words as well. Vocabulary words that are adjectives, verbs, or -ly adverbs may count as both when scoring if the adj, verb, or -ly adverb cards were one of the three chosen, so these words can be double points.

Sample: If a team chose simile, alliteration, and w-w clause, and the sentence on the board was *The king yelled*, they might write something like this:

> The king, who was perturbed and desperate, exploded like a violent volcano.

Scoring (Optional)

After the two minutes are up, each team must read their sentence. If they added all of their chosen elements correctly, they get 2 points for each.

Extra elements (from the eight or vocabulary), earn 2 extra points each.

Sample Scoring:

The sample sentence above uses all the required elements well (6 pts) plus it adds a vocabulary word (perturbed) and a strong verb (exploded), so they would receive 10 points. In this case, perturbed does not count double because adjective was not one of the chosen cards. (*Strong* verbs and *quality* adjectives are at the teacher's discretion.)

Repeat with more sentences. Here are some possibilities:

1. The dragon flew over the castle.

2. The knight hid behind a rock.

3. The princess danced all night.

4. The young man bowed before the king.

5. The peasant begged for mercy.

Find the Card for Vocabulary or Questions with Short Answers (a favorite!)

To prepare for vocabulary: Write each of the vocabulary words you wish to review on a separate note card. Spread them out face up on a table and let the students study them for no longer than one minute. Then turn them all face down. (In a large class, use larger cards and a pocket chart.)

To play, divide the class into three teams. Teams, in turn, do the following:

1. The teacher reads the definition of one of the words. The first team must turn over one of the word cards, trying to find the word that matches the definition.

2. If the word matches the definition, that team receives two points and the word card is returned to its spot on the table (face down) so that all word cards remain on the table the entire game. Play would then continue with the next team and the next definition.

3. If the word card does not match the definition, the word card is returned and the next team attempts to find the correct word for the same definition. Now the correct word is worth three points. If missed again, the next team tries for four points. Continue in this way until the correct word is found. Limit the point value to 10.

    Note: When an incorrect word is turned over, award one point if the team that picked it can give its correct definition.

4. Begin again with a new definition. Continue as above until all definitions have been used. The player or team with the most points wins.

For short answer questions, use questions instead of definitions, and put the answers on the cards.

Tic-Tac-Toe (or Connect Four)

Need: about twenty questions (Choose from pages 273–274.)
        a whiteboard OR paper and pencil
        two dice

1. Draw a tic-tac-toe board on a whiteboard or paper. Number the squares 1–9 in upper left corners.

2. Players are divided into an X team and an O team. They take turns trying to answer one of the questions. (You read one to them.)

3. If they answer correctly, place their X or O in the square of their choice. They then roll two dice.

4. The dice will determine whether they make special moves:

> *(Write this on the whiteboard for all to see.)*
>
> A total of 7 = Take an extra turn.
>
> Double 1, 2, or 3 = Erase an opponent's mark.
>
> Double 4, 5 = Erase an opponent's mark and replace it with yours.
>
> Double 6 = WILD. Go anywhere. (Can erase opponent if need be.)

5. Play until one team has three in a row or all squares are filled.

6. Repeat until one team has won two out of three or three out of five games.

For a longer game, try a 5 x 5 grid, and require four in a row to win.

21 QUESTIONS (or whatever number you desire)

To prepare:

1. Choose questions from the list below. (I usually choose 21.) Number each differently each time you play.

2. Write the numbers 1 through 21 (or however many questions you want to ask) on a whiteboard.

3. Obtain a die.

To Play:

1. Divide the class into three teams.

2. On each team's turn, they choose a number, and you read the corresponding question from your list. If a team answers correctly, they roll the die for points, and you erase the number from the board, so that question will not be chosen again.

3. If they answer incorrectly, you circle the number. The team gets no points. Now another team may choose that number for double points on their turn.

4. To add some fun, write "lose a turn" or "free roll" by two of your numbers.

5. Play until most questions have been chosen and teams have had an equal number of turns. Each player on the team with the most points receives five tickets.

QUESTIONS (You may renumber each time you play 21 Questions.)

1. What dress-ups have we learned thus far? How should you label them?

2. If you take a *who-which* clause out of a sentence, what should be left? *(a complete sentence)*

3. Give examples of 5 five-senses words, one for each sense. *(answers will vary)*

4. What do we call the time and place of a story? *(setting)*

5. What do we call the problem, want, or need of the main character of a story? *(conflict)*

6. In a story, what do we call the event that leads to the conflict being solved? *(climax)*

7. When punctuating conversation, periods and commas always go (*inside* or outside) end quotation marks.

8. What are the banned verbs? *(go, went, come, came, say, said, get, got, see, saw, look)*

9. What is alliteration? Give an example. *(three or more words that begin with the same <u>sound</u> (not necessarily letter) used close together: snow swept the city)*

10. What is a simile? Give an example. *(comparing one thing to another using* like *or* as: *She stood as still as a statue.)*

11. Where does a comma go with a *because* clause? *(after the because clause, unless there is a period there)*

12. What should each body paragraph of a report begin with? *(topic sentence)*

13. What should be highlighted in a topic sentence? *(key words that tell the topic)*

14. What should the clincher of a report paragraph do? *(repeat or reflect key words from the topic sentence)*

15. What is the topic sentence-clincher rule? *(The topic sentence and the clincher should repeat or reflect words that tell the topic of the paragraph. These words should be highlighted.)*

16. Do story paragraphs have topic sentences? *(no)*

17. How should you begin and end a 2- or 3-paragraph report? *(with sentences that tell the subject of the entire report—an introductory sentence and a final clincher)*

18. What are the banned adjectives? *(good, bad, pretty, ugly)*

19. What is a 3sss? *(three short, staccato sentences in a row)*

20. Where does a comma go with a www.asia.b clause? *(after the entire www.asia.b clause, unless there is a period there)*

21. What are the www.asia.b words? *(when, while, where, as, since, if, although, because)*

22. What is a fused outline? *(the outline you make after you take notes from more than one source; the outline you use to write a research report paragraph)*

23. When writing a research report (using more than one source text), after you have your sources, what must you know BEFORE you begin taking notes? *(topics)*

24. Should each note page for a research report have all the notes from the *same source* or all the notes for the *same topic*? *(same topic)* Why? *(so all notes for the same paragraph are together)*

25. What sentence openers have you learned? How do you label them?

26. Give six prepositions that can begin a #2 sentence. *(see SRN)*

27. When you must write without a source text (your own thoughts), how can you get ideas for what to say? *(ask yourself questions)*

28. What are the question starter words that can help you ask questions to think of more details to add to your writing? *(who, what, when, where, why, how, how feel, best thing, worst thing, describe)*

29. What is the structure of a 5-paragraph report? *(introduction, three body paragraphs, conclusion)*

30. What must an introduction paragraph include? *(grab attention, introduce the subject, give background, and introduce the topics of the body paragraphs)*

31. What must a concluding paragraph include? *(reflect the topics, tell what is most significant and why, end with a final clincher that reflects the opening)*

32. What is the purpose of a critique? *(to give and support an opinion about a story)*

33. What should you not say in a critique? *("I" or "my," as in "I think" or "In my opinion")*

34. What is a #5 sentence opener? *(www.asia.b clause)* What do these letters stand for? *(when, while, where, as, since, if, although, because)*

35. How would you describe a theme in literature? What are some common themes? *(a lesson, truth, or virtue taught, such as courage, love, diligence, determination)*

36. What should you have as the last page of a research report? *(bibliography)*

37. How many words may a very short sentence contain? *(2–5)*